MARK

—— OF THE ——

LEAST

Josh has been on a journey! Thankfully, he shares his experience with us. He has given us this book that searches the heart deeply, exposing the roots of the most insidious sin—pride. If God didn't tolerate pride in heaven, He certainly won't tolerate it in His church. What moves God's heart is finding a vessel humble enough to carry His presence without claiming His glory. When we forget where He found us, we risk losing where He placed us. This book touched me deeply. The fear of the Lord is the instruction of wisdom; and before honor is humility. Proverbs 15:33

—Thetus Tenney, author, speaker, and founder of World Network of Prayer

Josh Melancon hasn't just written about humility…he's lived it. I've personally watched him (with a front row seat) wrestle down ego, release old ambitions, and step into a leadership style rooted in surrender. *Mark of the Least* is not a theory book. It's truly a lived-out transformation. Every chapter carries the weight of someone who's been broken in all the right ways and has come through more grounded, more Christlike, and more usable in God's hands. If you're ready to stop performing and start becoming, this book will guide you there with conviction, compassion, and practical steps of growth.

—Ryan Franklin, Executive Coach and Author of *The Christian Leader Blueprint*

MARK

— OF THE —

LEAST

TRADING SELF-IMPORTANCE FOR
KINGDOM SIGNIFICANCE

JOSH MELANCON

MELANCON
MINISTRIES

First Edition

ISBN: 979-8-9990951-0-7 (hardcover)
ISBN: 979-8-9990951-1-4 (paperback)
ISBN: 979-8-9990951-2-1 (e-book)

For more information about the author or to schedule speaking engagements, visit www.melanconministries.com

Cover designer: Mandy Holloway

Interior Designer and Formatter: Dallas Hodge, dalhodge56@gmail.com

Publisher: Melancon Ministries, Thibodaux, Louisiana

Printed in the United States of America

"To bear His image is to carry the mark of the least."

FOREWORD

My friend Josh Melancon has a lot to be proud of. He's the husband of beautiful Keesha and the father of two capable young adults named Miley and Jensen. He's the visionary pastor of a rapidly growing church called House of Prayer that is impacting far beyond Thibodaux, LA. He's the son and successor of Bishop Ronnie Melancon, whose spiritual legacy is legendary. And he's a sought-after speaker for many meetings and a sought-out advisor for many leaders. As they say in preacher jargon, "He has corn in the crib." But you wouldn't know it to meet him, because he's just a humble, teachable guy that you would immediately like and instinctively trust. However, it wasn't always like that.

In this book, Pastor Josh recalls his early days in ministry and recounts some of the painful experiences that have powerfully shaped his perspective. And he reveals the sinister side of pride, courageously uncovering the misplaced motives that can derail any ministry, and transparently identifying the internal enemies that can decimate God's anointing in our lives. Because every leader knows all too well that sincere passion can easily be manipulated into polished performance, that being dedicated can quickly mutate into being driven, and that pushing for accomplishments can secretly morph into pandering for accolades. This is exactly why wise King Solomon wrote, "Above all else, guard your heart, for everything you do flows from it" (Proverbs 4:23 NIV).

For my friend, the journey to humility started with this compelling question from the Lord—"Son, you have heard of the mark of the beast, but have you heard of the mark of the least?" Along the way he admits that he has made some mistakes and suffered some setbacks, but most of all he has learned some very valuable lessons. And I'm so thankful that Pastor Josh is mature enough—and honest enough—to share them with us here.

The signposts along this road that is seldom travelled are marked with words that are seldom heard...Littleness, Lessness, Lastness, and

Leastness. Your ego may resist taking the trip, but your spirit will be renewed and your ministry will be revitalized if you decide to make the journey. This book will be your reliable road map. Each chapter is filled with profound insights and ends with penetrating questions that will help you utilize and internalize these truths. And by the time you finish walking through these pages with my friend, your heart will be forever imprinted with "The Mark of the Least."

Raymond Woodward
Fredericton, NB

TABLE OF CONTENTS

To my parents, Ronnie and Rhonda Melancon—
thank you for teaching me that humility isn't weakness but strength.

Your quiet example of leastness shaped
my understanding of kingdom greatness.

The pages that follow were born from
the life you lived before I understood it.

INTRODUCTION

Writing a book on humility is a challenge in itself. After all, who can honestly say they've mastered such a demanding virtue? At first glance, humility isn't even appealing. It suggests plainness—something easy to overlook or dismiss.

For years, I struggled with humility. My journey began with a relentless pursuit of excellence, an unquenchable hunger to outperform and outshine others in every arena. Competitiveness flowed through my veins, driving me to set ever-higher achievement goals. My ultimate aim was to be unbeatable and unmatched in all endeavors. This endless striving produced an illusion of progress, but rewarded disappointment.

Instead of satisfaction, I found myself stuck in a quicksand of anxiety and frustration. With each goal reached, my restlessness seemed to deepen, rather than bringing the satisfaction I expected. I worked harder, gave more, and still came up short.

Even as I reached and surpassed every lofty target I set, an empty victory echoed in my accomplishment gallery. The triumphs I envisioned as sources of fulfillment left me feeling discontented. A troubling sense of wrongness persisted, whispering that I had somehow lost my way along this ambitious path.

As I looked back through my life's highlight reel, a pattern appeared, one that I was too blind to see. Despite the natural talent that turned heads and the drive that pushed me to excel, I fell short with a regularity that stung. Something always tripped me on the last hurdle. Second place became my common companion.

Then came the crowning moment of my high school basketball career, the state championship. We made history that night, securing our school's first title. I sat in the back of my friend's Blazer, clutching the net we had cut down after the winning shot. Unexpected emptiness crept in. This is it? The question hit fast, and just like that, the victory didn't feel like a win.

All those years of grinding, all that striving, and this was it? That quiet disappointment was God's first gentle tug—pulling at a thread I didn't yet know was unraveling everything I believed about success.

My pattern of near-misses revealed an inescapable truth: God wasn't waiting for me to succeed—He was waiting for me to surrender. Until I let go, breakthroughs stayed just out of reach. But when I finally did, doors didn't just open, they blew out. That's when I realized the problem wasn't the race itself. It was the way I was running it. I had chased success, but missed surrender. That had to change.

It wasn't distance from the struggle that brought me clarity, though. I had to wrestle with it long enough to see what I'd missed. At last, my search revealed Proverbs 25:2: "It is God's privilege to conceal things and the king's privilege to discover them" (NLT).

God had hidden the very thing I was missing; only those with eyes to see—those who had reached the end of themselves and were ready to discover true strength in surrender—could perceive it. Over and over, humility shows up in Scripture. Quiet. Steady. Foundational. Not just in leaders, but in everyone God called. Rarely the headline, but always a part of the story. All true greatness rests on humility as its invisible cornerstone. It's not a personality trait. It's the bedrock of authentic power. Our eyes focus on outward qualities such as charisma, talent, and boldness, but humility supports everything visible.

I had chased breakthrough through effort and achievement, thinking that if I worked hard enough, success would follow. But God wasn't asking me to strive—He was asking me to surrender. And surrender, I learned, is impossible without humility. We treat humility like a secondary virtue—quiet, passive, maybe even weak. But in God's economy, it's the foundation. Without it, even the best intentions drift off course.

Moses didn't step into leadership with swagger—he hesitated. At the burning bush, he questioned everything about himself: "Who am I that I should go to Pharaoh?" God didn't scold him for doubting. Instead, He anchored Moses in something greater: "I will be with you." That moment wasn't about Moses proving himself. It was about letting go.

Surrender, not strength, forms the foundation of God's call. A lesson I had yet to learn. Humility doesn't come easy—especially in a world obsessed with platforms, profiles, and proving your worth. It feels like stepping backward when everything around you says push forward. But that's the paradox: The lower you go, the stronger your foundation becomes. The more you let go—of ego, control, recognition—the more God can build in you what you couldn't build for yourself. It's not flashy. It's not loud. But it holds when everything else breaks.

Jesus didn't just teach humility—He walked it out. He flipped the world's definition of greatness on its head. His strength was quiet. His power surrendered. Influence didn't come from grabbing a platform, but from laying Himself down. The more I've studied His life—and wrestled with my own—the clearer it's become: Leastness isn't weakness. It's the way of the kingdom.

> **Humility is not the virtue we choose when all else fails. It is the foundation that prevents all else from failing.**

In the book of Matthew, Jesus said: "Take my yoke upon you, and learn of me; for I am meek and lowly in heart: and ye shall find rest unto your souls" (Matthew 11:29 KJV).

This tells us rest is tied to humility—which means pride can only lead to restlessness. We search for peace in all the wrong places: in more stuff, louder platforms, and bigger names. But the soul doesn't find rest in striving. It finds rest in surrender.

Humility isn't about thinking less of yourself. It's about thinking of yourself less. It's not self-rejection—it's freedom from self-importance. And that freedom doesn't come easy. Like a miner digging through layers of rock, we have to chip away at pride, ego, and fear to find what's buried deep: a humility that holds. It's not flashy, but it's worth everything. This isn't a onetime dig. It's daily. The kind of journey that shapes more than our character—it shapes our calling.

"Likewise, ye younger, submit yourselves unto the elder. Yea, all of you be subject one to another, and be clothed with humility: for God resisteth the proud, and giveth grace to the humble" (1 Peter 5:5 KJV).

We talk often about the garments of praise, the robe of righteousness, even the armor of God. But how often do we speak of the one garment Jesus Himself wore openly—humility? I had chased every other one: the mantle of leadership, the cloak of anointing, even the crown of achievement. But this? This was the one I had overlooked. True authority in God's kingdom doesn't come from reaching higher—it comes from kneeling lower. Real influence doesn't rise from ambition. It flows through surrender.

Like Joseph in Pharaoh's prison, I learned that what felt like setback was setup. Every stripping down was God preparing me for the only garment that attracts heaven's favor. When we clothe ourselves with humility, we're wearing the uniform of kingdom authority.

This journey has surprised me. I'm not climbing higher. I'm learning to go lower. And every time God calls me deeper, it requires me to become smaller. My flesh fights for justification, for control, for victory—but God's whisper keeps cutting through the noise: "Let go. Step back. Decrease."

"He must increase, but I must decrease" (John 3:30 KJV).

That is my war. That is my worship. That is my way forward.

And it has brought me to this one truth: To bear His image is to carry the mark of the least.

CHAPTER 1:

LEASTNESS

"Yet it shall not be so among you; but whoever desires to become great among you shall be your servant. And whoever of you desires to be first shall be slave of all."

Mark 10:43–44 NKJV

I had finally done it—I preached to a crowd of more than 1,200 people. This was a milestone, a sign that I had "made it" as a minister. As my wife, Keesha, drove us home, I slouched beside her in silence so quiet it hurt. What should have been my crowning moment left me feeling unsettled. Why did this well-received sermon leave me feeling unfulfilled and unimportant? Instead of feeling accomplished, I felt hollow. The very thing I had convinced myself would bring fulfillment left me embarrassed by the shallowness of my aspirations.

With an unexpected suddenness, the Lord's presence filled the car with a solemn intensity. I knew He wanted to speak, and I was willing to listen. His words changed everything:

"Son, you have heard of the mark of the beast, but have you heard of the mark of the least?"

Divine Disruption

Though I didn't fully grasp what He meant in that moment, I felt the weight of His words settle on my spirit. I had been chasing society's markers—success, fame, fortune—believing they would validate my ministry. But in truth, they had become my secret temptations, my hidden motivations. Until that moment, I hadn't recognized just how much they had a grip on me.

The beast's mark represents submission to a broken, godless system. But the mark God was showing me—a mark I had completely overlooked—was different. It wasn't about accolades or crowds. It was about humility. About surrender. About serving others in quiet obedience. God was revealing that true greatness in His kingdom doesn't come from being recognized, but from being refined.

In that moment, I realized I had been enrolled in God's school of leastness. And over the next few years, He would reshape everything I thought I knew about ministry. While I had been chasing platforms and positions—all under the banner of "answering the call"—God was forming something different in me: a heart willing to be unseen, a life willing to be poured out.

While the current culture pushes people to seek status and power— as if those things can be controlled and directed without destructive consequences—God's people carry a different mark. It's not a badge worn outwardly but an invisible imprint etched into the heart. This identity isn't about future prophecy; it's about present posture. It shows up when we choose to decrease so others can increase, when we find joy in supporting roles, when we celebrate others' successes, embrace invisible service, and take the lower seat without resentment.

> While the world craves visibility and applause, heaven esteems something else entirely.

The truly remarkable are those who understand this upside-down reality: In Christ's kingdom, the way up is down. True influence flows not from platform, but from posture. Authentic greatness is measured not by how many serve us, but by how faithfully we serve.

This mark of humility becomes our most significant distinction. In God's kingdom, the least become the greatest, the last become first, the invisible become unforgettable, and the servants become royalty. This divine reversal challenges every worldly metric of success. Jesus made it clear: Greatness isn't measured by how high we climb, but by how low we're willing to bow in service to others.

Even now, writing these words brings a sense of shame. The revelation still cuts deep. I had twisted God's sacred calling into a platform for self-glorification, masking raw ambition beneath spiritual language. As Keesha drove in silence, I sat stunned—convicted by the contrast between what I wanted and what God intended. Between building *my* kingdom and serving *His.*

That moment marked the beginning of my education in leastness—a slow, often uncomfortable journey that would redefine my understanding of ministry and undo much of what I thought I knew about serving God. What started as a painful confrontation became the first unlocking of my divine purpose through holy humility.

The words of Luke 9:48 KJV—"Who is least among you will be great"—became my compass. That mysterious truth launched a new pursuit: not of visibility or acclaim, but of significance through surrender.

Leastness is often something we feel before we understand. It washes over us in moments of humility—sometimes through circumstances we didn't choose, other times through decisions we didn't expect to make. It's that unmistakable sense of being small, of feeling diminished. Still, I've learned this: Even in moments that sting, humility gives us the strength to accept being overlooked without losing who we are.

That truth was tested in a pivotal ministry moment. While I was serving alongside a close friend, our church began seeking a new student pastor. Having taught the student Bible study for several years, I naturally assumed I was next in line. Instead, my father—the senior pastor—appointed my friend to the position.

In that moment, the waters of leastness rose around me. I faced a critical decision: resist the descent or embrace it. By God's grace, I chose the latter. Rather than assert what I thought I deserved, I acknowledged my friend's readiness—and recognized my own need for continued growth.

I could have justified entitlement. *"I've put in the work." "I've been teaching for years." "I've earned this."* But instead, God invited me into something quieter and harder: to prefer my friend's advancement over my own, and to champion his leadership rather than compete with it.

So I made a decision that felt counterintuitive. I discontinued my separate Bible study and encouraged my students to unite with his. What looked like surrender turned into multiplication. The unified group thrived, and today, we both pastor flourishing churches.

Looking back, I see how that single act of embracing leastness preserved something far more valuable than a temporary title. Had I clung to wounded pride, I might have fractured a friendship—or forfeited my future ministry. But what felt like diminishment became a doorway to lasting kingdom impact.

Reflecting on that experience, I still feel a wave of embarrassment when I think about the prideful attitudes that had taken root in my heart. But that moment in the car—when God spoke and my disappointment finally quieted me enough to hear Him—marked the beginning of something deeper. I stopped making excuses. I stopped justifying my ambition. That night became the starting point of trading self-importance for kingdom significance.

God made it clear: He wasn't after the version of greatness I had been chasing. He was calling me to a different mark—the one He'd whispered to my heart during that long drive home. That question stayed with me, exposing how much I had confused ministry success with spiritual maturity.

What I had labeled as "answering the call" had become a convenient cover for ungodly pursuits. But in that car, God shifted the standard. He brought me back to Luke 9:48 NLT: "He who is least among you will be great." From that moment on, I committed to pursue greatness—not through platforms and visibility, but through a surrendered posture of leastness before the Lord.

Until that point, I hadn't even considered "leastness" a real word— much less the pathway to true kingdom influence. But as I began to surrender my ego and let go of my self-serving desires, I caught my first glimpse of what fulfillment actually looks like: humble, Christ-centered service. That became the mark I began to chase—the imprint I desired to bear as one of God's chosen.

We encounter leastness in those moments that shrink us—when we're unseen, passed over, or stretched beyond what we thought we could handle. It's that unsettling sense of being small or overlooked. And yet, something sacred happens there.

Even in that low place, there's a quiet strength. A grounded confidence that comes not from pride, but from surrender. It's the kind of strength that lets you absorb belittlement without letting it define you.

These weren't ideas I learned from a leadership book or picked up in a seminary lecture. They were etched into my heart by example—through the life my parents lived in front of me.

In 1984, my parents became pastors of a small, unassuming church. There was no salary, no prestige, and no promise of "greater opportunities" on the other side. But they didn't view that assignment as beneath them. They embraced it as holy.

Where others may have seen a stepping stone, they saw a divine invitation. And what I witnessed in their approach changed how I understood ministry. They modeled something radically countercultural: They chose downward mobility—not because they lacked options, but because they knew what mattered to God.

They weren't chasing titles or platforms. They were chasing Jesus. And because of that, they saw things others missed. They found meaning in places others dismissed. Their choice to walk humbly—and to keep walking when it was hard—positioned them for the kind of fruitfulness only God can produce.

That living example continues to shape me. They taught me that God's highest callings don't always come wrapped in prestige. Often, they come dressed in obscurity and disguised as ordinary. And if we're not paying attention—if we're too focused on what looks impressive—we'll miss them.

This living demonstration shaped my understanding in ways no platform ever could. My parents showed me that humble people don't miss divine opportunities just because those opportunities seem small. Lowly people—willing to take lowly assignments—are the ones who often walk in God's highest purposes.

They didn't choose that path because there were no other alternatives. They chose it because they recognized that some of God's greatest gifts are wrapped in simplicity—and sometimes in suffering. That awareness changed me. It continues to remind me to stay watchful: to avoid chasing the approval of people or measuring success by applause. Because when we let those things guide us, we're in danger of missing the very things God has prepared for us.

> His blessings don't always come dressed in honor.

They rarely arrive with recognition. More often, they look like inconvenience. Sacrifice. Obscurity. And if we're not careful, we'll walk right past them in search of something shinier.

Let this not deter you. When we hunger for the things of God and choose the path of humility, He helps us see past the "ugly wrappings" to the joy and fulfillment waiting on the other side. The humble road may not be easy, but it leads to the kind of transformation we can't find anywhere else.

Jesus modeled this perfectly. He endured the cross and "despised the shame" because His identity was rooted in the Father—not in the opinions of the crowd. He didn't spend His life trying to impress people or protect an image. He walked in quiet confidence, fully surrendered to His mission.

That's what humility produces: freedom.

When we're no longer trapped by the need for approval, we're free to follow God fully—regardless of the cost. The labels and expectations of this world lose their grip, and we're finally able to run after the purposes of God without hesitation or fear.

I've chosen to move from hiding behind a polished image to humbly accepting every part of my story—even the hard parts—as part of God's plan. In comparison to the emptiness and dissatisfaction I once felt chasing the unattainable, this path has been worth it. It hasn't been easy—yours won't be either—but it has been fulfilling.

True humility isn't about shrinking back or pretending we have nothing to offer. It's about seeing ourselves clearly, knowing who we are in God and living from that place. We aren't self-made or self-sustained. Everything we have—our talents, opportunities, insight—is a gift. We are deeply loved and completely dependent.

When we understand our position before God, it recalibrates everything. We stop striving to prove something and start walking in steady grace. Humility allows us to hold both realities at once: We are created in God's image and called to His purpose, yet we are also desperately in need of His mercy every day. That balance helps us live with both confidence and reverence—embracing our divine worth while staying anchored in dependence on the One who formed us.

When it comes to others, genuine humility means understanding we're not above or beneath anyone. We all carry unique gifts and wounds. Humility allows us to celebrate someone else's success without feeling threatened, to serve without resentment, and to ask for help without shame.

It means we don't have to pretend we're perfect, or act like we have it all together. We can admit where we're weak, own our mistakes, and still walk with healthy confidence. That's the kind of balance humility brings: not insecurity, not pride, but a steady awareness that we all need grace.

This posture frees us from the exhausting extremes of arrogance on one side and self-doubt on the other. It helps us engage with others from a place of genuine equality and mutual respect as fellow image-bearers of God.

This balanced perspective is what true humility looks like. Both Rick Warren and C. S. Lewis, writing decades apart and from different cultural contexts, arrived at the same profound insight about the nature of true humility.

Warren, writing in twenty-first-century America for a contemporary Christian audience, cuts through modern misconceptions about humility with his memorable distinction: "Humility is not thinking less of yourself; it's thinking of yourself less." His phrasing speaks directly to a culture obsessed with self-esteem and personal worth, clarifying that humility isn't about self-deprecation or diminished self-regard.[i]

Lewis, writing in 1940s Britain during and after World War II, expressed the identical truth through his characteristic philosophical precision: "A truly humble man…will not be thinking about humility: he will not be thinking about himself at all." His observation captures the same essence—that genuine humility transcends self-focus entirely.[ii]

The consistency of this insight across time and culture suggests something universal about human nature—that our natural tendency toward self-absorption is the real barrier to humility, and that true freedom comes not from thinking about ourselves differently, but from thinking about ourselves less frequently altogether.

---

i Rick Warren, *The Purpose Driven Life: What on Earth Am I Here For?* (Grand Rapids, MI: Zondervan, 2002), 21.

ii *C. S. Lewis, Mere Christianity* (New York: Macmillan, 1952), 128.

It frees us to be honest about our strengths and weaknesses without needing to prove our worth or hide our flaws.

My version of pride was more subtle—always positioning myself to be the dominant voice, the expert in the room. Like Stan Gleason described in *Follow to Lead*, I had embraced a "Here I am" posture rather than a "There you are" mindset.[iii]

Every environment became a stage. Every conversation, an audition. I wasn't just contributing—I was competing. I was constantly trying to demonstrate my value, to say the most insightful thing, to highlight my knowledge. I lived in a constant state of performance—always needing to show I belonged, always trying to prove I was valuable.

I felt the pressure to be the smartest voice in the room, the expert on every subject, the one with the final word. It wasn't confidence; it was survival. I had learned how to present as polished and articulate, all while hiding a deep fear that I wasn't enough.

That kind of pride doesn't look aggressive—it looks polished. But it's still pride. The spirit of rejection had twisted my God-given intelligence into a shield, something I used to guard myself and keep others from discovering my flaws. I wasn't comfortable enough with my perceived defects to let people get close, to let them rub against my imperfections. Rather than allowing that, I chose to stay guarded. Instead of using my voice to build connection, I used it to stay in control.

The critical spirit that accompanied this pride was relentless. Nothing escaped my evaluation. Every decision became something to dissect, every idea something to critique. I had convinced myself it was discernment—but the truth was, I was just uncomfortable letting go.

Admitting this still makes me cringe. But owning our past is part of stepping into healing.

As God began His work in me, I started to see a different way. Humble people listen more than they speak. They seek to understand before they try to be understood. They show mercy before they rush to judgment. They offer gentleness instead of criticism—and they're not afraid to take the lowest seat in the room.

---

iii Stan Gleason, *Follow to Lead: The Journey of a Disciple Maker* (Hazelwood, MO: Pentecostal Publishing House, 2016).

Servant Leadership: Power Through Service

Simon Sinek's *Leaders Eat Last* champions "servant leadership," the practice of putting a team's needs ahead of one's own. The book's title borrows a military custom—officers eating only after their soldiers—to illustrate how genuine leaders place themselves last.

As Sinek explains, "leaders who are willing to eat last are rewarded with deeply loyal colleagues who will stop at nothing to advance their leader's vision," and that leadership is "a choice, not a rank—available to anyone willing to look out for the person on your left and the person on your right."

His "Circle of Safety" concept calls leaders to create environments in which team members feel protected and valued, setting aside self-interest so others can thrive. Such service-first leadership proves that those who serve most often lead best.[iv]

That was the invitation: to stop defending my ego and start reflecting His heart.

Authentic leadership isn't about being the most capable person in the room. It's about being the most willing to serve. It's not a posture of weakness—it's a choice to be more concerned with the needs of others than with securing your own position.

Unlearning the Climb

God's healing in my heart has been nothing short of transformational—a divine reversal of what I now recognize as the pride I once carried. He's teaching me that real strength often means stepping back. That true wisdom knows when to stay silent. That authentic leadership serves first. And that lasting influence is rooted in humility, not ambition.

This upside-down wisdom has changed the way I lead, the way I relate, and the way I see myself. I no longer feel the need to prove something or perform for approval. The striving has been replaced with surrender. Most surprising is that in this surrender, I've found freedom— freedom in becoming less so that Christ might become more through me.

---

iv Simon Sinek, *Leaders Eat Last: Why Some Teams Pull Together and Others Don't* (New York: Portfolio, 2014).

The journey from perpetual expert to willing learner, from constant critic to grateful participant, hasn't been easy. But the shift from "Here I am" to "There you are" has brought a freedom I didn't know I needed.

Philippians 2:3–4 NIV says it plainly: "Do nothing out of selfish ambition or vain conceit. Rather, in humility value others above yourselves, not looking to your own interests but each of you to the interests of the others."

The effectiveness of our prayer lives isn't measured by what happens in the prayer room. It's revealed in how we live outside of it. If pride isn't broken in God's presence, it will break our relationships in His absence.

That time in prayer should shape the way we speak, listen, forgive, and lead. It should produce gentleness in our tone, wisdom in our words, and grace in our reactions. What happens vertically must be reflected horizontally—otherwise it's incomplete.

True transformation requires a willingness to be accountable—to invite correction, own mistakes, and stay honest about where we still need to grow. It means listening to trusted voices, apologizing quickly, and resisting the urge to overestimate our spiritual maturity.

That kind of humility creates good soil. It guards us from the self-deception that often grows alongside spiritual pride, and it makes room for honest feedback—the kind that doesn't just affirm us, but actually shapes us into Christ's image instead of the idealized version of ourselves we're tempted to project.

Satan's strategy isn't always to stop us from serving God—sometimes it's to distort *how* we serve. We say yes to the call, but quietly carry the world's ambitions with us. We want the biggest church. The most recognition. The fastest growth. And sometimes, even the desire to win souls can get tangled in pride if our motives aren't checked.

It's possible to pursue godly goals with selfish ambition—doing the right thing for the wrong reason. That's the danger of pride: It doesn't just show up in rebellion. It shows up in ministry. And when it does, our calling gets corrupted, driven not by the Spirit, but by the need to prove ourselves.

Sometimes, God's "next" isn't greater—it's smaller.

It's not the promotion we imagined but the step down we didn't expect. Humility understands that downward paths can lead to greater glory, smaller platforms can bear more fruit, and hidden roles can carry deeper purpose. That's the paradox of the kingdom: The way up is down, and true significance often hides in what the world calls insignificant.

In God's economy, advancement often requires descent. Growth doesn't start when we climb higher—it begins when we choose to lower ourselves. Real maturity shows up when we elevate others, even when it costs us visibility.

Authentic leadership, grounded in humility, asks different questions:

- Not "Could I?" but "Should I?"

- Not "Will this advance me?" but "Is this God's door?"

- Not "What will I gain?" but "What does God want?"

- Not "How will this look?" but "How will this serve?"

There's strength in setting limits—in saying no to opportunities that might elevate your platform but diminish your purpose. Some doors lead to applause but not obedience. Some roles boost your status but shrink your soul. True kingdom discernment doesn't chase what looks good; it follows what *is* good—what God wants.

I've seen this lived out in our church. Men choosing obedience over optics. Taking lower-paying jobs to answer a calling. Moving to smaller homes to make room for mission. Driving older cars so they could give more generously. Stepping down to step up in God's kingdom.

The world sees those decisions as loss. But I've watched these men walk in peace that defies logic, joy that money can't buy, and fulfillment no status can offer. Their lives are living proof of Christ's upside-down kingdom—where surrender leads to freedom, sacrifice brings abundance, and the path of leastness leads to the greatest treasure of all: intimate fellowship with the One who emptied Himself completely so we could be filled with His presence.

Are you anxious about the future? Stressed about what you're becoming? Caught up in trying to figure out the next big step?

Let me tell you what I wish I had known earlier: I needed to loosen the stranglehold I had on timing, image, and success. Trying to control every outcome chokes the life out of a calling. I had almost destroyed mine before I realized that being whole in Christ required a change in who was in charge. And it wasn't me.

There's no need to force an outcome through manipulation. No reason to obsess over what must be achieved or how it will happen. When you focus on walking with God and obeying His voice, you'll find yourself exactly where you need to be, exactly when you need to be there.

Here's what I've learned through wrong turns, missteps, and missed opportunities: God factors in our flaws. He's not thrown off by our detours—in fact, He weaves them into His plan. So let go of the fear of failure, the pressure to perform, the need to control, and the urge to prove yourself. Your worth isn't tied to your productivity. It's anchored in your identity—as someone deeply loved and fully accepted by God.

You don't have to make it happen. You just have to walk with Him. Obey Him. Trust Him. Rest in His timing. Most spiritual breakthroughs aren't marked by dramatic moments, but by the quiet, daily choice to keep placing one foot in front of the other on the path He's marked for you.

Coming Full Circle

Today, when I look back at that car ride—the silence, the confusion, the hollow feeling that followed what should have been a triumphant moment—I see it differently. That wasn't the end of something. It was the beginning. The moment God interrupted my striving and invited me into surrender.

He didn't ask for perfection. He asked for my attention.

He didn't shame me. He shaped me.

He didn't reject me. He redirected me.

That's the beauty of grace. Even when we're chasing the wrong things, God meets us in the middle of our mess. He marks us—not for status, but for servanthood. Only when we allow His imprint will everything begin to change.

Discussion Questions for Chapter 1: Leastness

Let's Start Here:

Before diving deep, take a moment to appreciate someone whose quiet impact shaped your journey.

Who's someone in your life who made a meaningful difference without seeking recognition or praise?

It could be:

- A teacher or mentor who believed in you when you didn't believe in yourself

- Someone who did the behind-the-scenes work that helped you succeed

- A friend or family member who quietly supported your dreams

- A coworker who always helped but never expected the credit

- A person whose small act of kindness came at just the right time

In this chapter, we're exploring what it means to live as "the least." Reflecting on those who've modeled that for us is a good place to begin.

1. When Success Feels Empty

Josh described feeling hollow and unfulfilled after preaching to a crowd of more than 1,200 people—what should have been a defining moment in his ministry.

- Why do you think getting what we thought we wanted can still leave us empty?

- Can you think of a time when something you achieved didn't bring the satisfaction you expected?

2. The Mark of the Least vs. the Mark of the Beast

In the car that day, God interrupted Josh's thoughts with the question, *"You've heard of the mark of the beast—but have you heard of the mark of the least?"*

- How do these two "marks" show up in everyday life?
- What does it actually look like to walk in leastness in a culture obsessed with influence, image, and upward mobility?

3. "Here I Am" vs. "There You Are"

He writes about shifting from always needing to be the smartest person in the room to becoming someone focused on truly seeing and serving others.

- How can you tell when someone is stuck in "here I am" mode versus showing genuine humility?
- Where are you most tempted to prove yourself instead of simply being present and helpful?

4. Going Down Instead of Up

This chapter tells stories of people who took pay cuts, moved to smaller homes, or drove older cars in order to obey God's leading.

- What does it say about a person's heart when they're willing to go backward in the world's eyes to follow God?
- Is there an opportunity in front of you that might boost your status but shrink your soul?

Further Reflection

The Upside-Down Way

Josh's journey shows that the more he tried to control outcomes, chase status, and prove himself, the more frustrated and unfulfilled he became. But when he began to release control and embrace a lower path, he found clarity, purpose, and peace.

- How does this idea—that spiritual growth often comes through surrender, humility, and unseen faithfulness—challenge your definition of success?

- What would shift in your mindset or lifestyle if you truly believed that choosing to be least leads to God's best?

CHAPTER 2:
DIVINE IMPRINTS

"But we have this treasure in earthen vessels, that the excellence of the power may be of God and not of us."

2 Corinthians 4:7 NKJV

Jesus chose rough wood and hard labor—the texture of humanity pressed into divinity.

The very Creator who spoke galaxies into existence stepped into the tools and trade of ordinary men. The Architect of the universe took up the work of a builder, His divine power wrapped in calloused fingers. Jesus didn't just visit humanity—He entered fully into our mess. Then embraced us. He chose the daily grind of our existence and the limitations of flesh.

Philippians 2:6–8 NIV captures it perfectly: "Who, being in very nature God, did not consider equality with God something to be used to his own advantage; rather, he made himself nothing by taking the very nature of a servant, being made in human likeness. And being found in appearance as a man, he humbled himself by becoming obedient to death—even death on a cross!"

Where David confessed our fallen nature—"I was shapen in iniquity; and in sin did my mother conceive me" (Psalm 51:5 KJV)—Jesus stepped into that fallen world on purpose. He met us in the mess, not requiring us to rise to Him, but coming down to us.

Life leaves a mark. Whether shaped by our choices or by circumstances we never saw coming, those marks do something to us. They push us in one of two directions: We either stay wounded or we become scarred—and stronger. The difference isn't in the pain itself, but in how we respond to it.

Too often, we choose the path of wounded existence. I've done it—I've tried to overcompensate, to prove I wasn't weak, to outrun the pain. Maybe you have too. We fight to rise above our own shame by controlling others. We scan every relationship for threats, constantly on edge, expecting rejection. We apply temporary fixes to deep wounds—things like success, sex, status, or substance. We numb out through addiction or distraction, doing whatever it takes to avoid feeling broken.

But healing doesn't come through avoidance. It begins with a different kind of courage—the willingness to slow down and face our pain, not with harsh judgment, but with honesty and reflection. To sit with it long enough to let God offer us perspective and perception.

It's in that stillness, that quiet pause, where transformation begins—where wounds, once feared or hidden, start to become something more.

Instead of staying stuck in cycles of avoidance, denial, or numbing, we can follow the path marked by sacred scars. It's a path chosen by those willing to embrace transformation. Rather than running from pain, we face it with honesty. What once felt like punishment becomes a teacher. Shame softens into compassion. Suffering, when placed in God's hands, no longer isolates—it connects.

It comes through entrusting it to the One who redeems every broken place. The scars remain, but they no longer signal defeat. They declare survival. Overcoming. Grace.

> **True healing doesn't come by pretending the pain doesn't exist.**

These sacred marks become living proof: What tried to destroy us didn't. That healing is possible. That God still turns wounds into wisdom and stories into light for others still walking through the dark. Scars become credentials, testifying not just to our pain, but to our redemption.

Psalm 41:11 KJV reads: "By this I know that thou favourest me, because mine enemy doth not triumph over me." This verse reminds us that while the enemy may strike, he doesn't win. When we turn to God, even the marks meant to harm us become evidence of His favor.

God doesn't promise a life free of pain. Out of love, He allows us—and others—the freedom to choose. And sometimes, those choices leave a mark. But He *does* promise redemption. In His hands, the wounds that were meant to break us become part of a greater story of grace. They become witnesses.

The question isn't whether we'll be marked. If you're breathing, you already have been. The question is what those marks will become. Will they remain open wounds, raw and unresolved? Or will they become sacred scars—signs of survival, redemption, and grace?

> By God's calculations, value increases through surrender, not success.

He doesn't invest His treasures in those who seem the strongest by human standards—He places them in broken vessels. He transforms weakness into strength and raises up the lowly to display His power.

God often chooses the ones who have been marked—scarred by life, emptied of pride, and humbled by experience—to launch His greatest movements. His ways upend the world's logic. The very people who seem least likely, the ones who've been bruised and broken, become the vessels of His greatest work. Why? Because they have nothing left to prove. Their strength doesn't come from self, but from Him.

This is the genius of God's investment strategy: He uses what the world would discard. He multiplies impact through those who no longer rely on themselves. In the kingdom of God, spiritual bankruptcy becomes the currency of transformation.

Get on Your Mark: From Wounds to Wisdom

Every divine imprint carries intention, and every scar tells a story of transformation. As Paul declared in Galatians 6:17 KJV, "I bear in my body the marks of the Lord Jesus"—not as symbols of shame, but as signposts of grace.

Your path is marked with purpose. "I press toward the mark," Paul writes in Philippians 3:14 KJV. That's not just about moving forward; it's about moving intentionally. Each experience—painful or triumphant—serves as a divine coordinate on your journey. Pride turns those markers into stumbling blocks. However, humility recognizes them as sacred ground. These aren't punishments—they're purposeful. When humility guides your steps, even the worst experiences become milestones on the road to your destiny.

> If you run from your pain, you'll miss your starting line.

Healing doesn't begin by avoiding the wound—it starts when we embrace it. Our wounds, when handed over to the Master Surgeon, become wisdom. Our failures, when faced, become foundations. "I run in the path of your commands, for you have broadened my understanding" (Psalm 119:32 NIV).

God uses every tear, trial, and triumph to align you with His design. Your scars aren't random—they're sacred. They mark where His grace met your pain. The deepest wounds often point to your highest calling. And a heart that's been healed becomes a heart that understands.

> Scripture paints a stark contrast between two kinds of marks—one of allegiance to darkness, and the other revealing a belonging to the Father and His divine purpose.

In the book of Revelation, chapter 13, verses 16–17 KJV, we are painted a vivid picture: "And he causeth all, both small and great, rich and poor, free and bond, to receive a mark in their right hand, or in their foreheads: And that no man might buy or sell, save he that had the mark."

Now contrast this with the seal of God's people in Revelation 7:3 KJV: "Hurt not the earth...till we have sealed the servants of our God in their foreheads." And again in Revelation 14:1 KJV: "A Lamb stood on the mount Sion, and with him an hundred forty and four thousand, having his Father's name written in their foreheads."

The contrast is notable. The beast's mark reflects a system of pride, control, and self-exaltation. God's seal reflects humility, surrender, and identity in Christ. The mark of the beast enables advancement on a selfish level. The mark of the Father often leads to obscurity, sacrifice, and the way of downward mobility.

That's because the mark of God is not a static stamp—it's a living seal. It deepens through trials, becomes visible through service, and is strengthened by submission. It shows up in daily choices, in quiet obedience, in selfless love.

This seal of humility isn't a symbol without representation. It's a lifestyle. And it sets us apart in a world obsessed with self. The choice of which mark we bear.

Discussion Questions for Chapter 2: Divine Imprints

Let's Start Here:

God chose uncut stones for His altars—not the polished or perfect ones. Sometimes, our "mess-ups" end up being meaningful.

Can you think of a time when something imperfect turned out even better than what you originally planned?

Maybe it was:

- A recipe that flopped but became a family favorite
- A project that didn't go as expected but looked even better
- A speech or performance where forgetting your plan made it more real
- A wrong turn that led to an unforgettable adventure

Let's celebrate the beauty in life's "happy accidents"—those moments where imperfection became a blessing.

1. Wounded vs. Scarred

The chapter says life's tough stuff marks your soul, and you get to choose: stay wounded or let God turn those hurts into sacred scars.

- What's the difference between staying wounded and being scarred-but-healing?
- Can you think of a time when you had to decide between holding on to pain or letting God use it to make you stronger?

2. God Likes Broken Things

The author talks about how God wanted altars made from naturally broken stones, not perfectly cut ones.

- What do you think it means to be "perfectly broken" in God's eyes?
- How does that challenge the idea that we need to "get it all together" before we come to Him?

3. Humility's Mark vs. The World's Mark

The chapter contrasts the mark of the beast (pride and power) with God's seal of humility.

- What might it look like to live with "the mark of humility" today?
- How could that kind of humility cost you something in worldly terms?

4. Leading from Your Scars

The author says real leadership comes from caring about others—not from chasing status or recognition.

- How have your own struggles or pain shaped the way you show up for others?
- What's the difference between leading to impress and leading to serve?

5. God's "Unlikely" Choices

The chapter asks why God so often picks broken, humble people—not the obvious superstars.

- How are "broken vessels" usually viewed in today's culture?
- Is there something about you—something that feels weak or small—that God might actually want to use?

CHAPTER 3:

THE MARK THAT MADE ME

*"To console those who mourn in Zion, to give them beauty for ashes,
the oil of joy for mourning, the garment of praise for the spirit of
heaviness; that they may be called trees of righteousness, the planting
of the Lord, that He may be glorified."*

Isaiah 61:3 NKJV

From the beginning, leastness marked me. My parents turned a rundown trailer—once used as Sunday school rooms—into our home. Sitting behind a small church, my childhood home sported sagging floors, falling insulation, window units that strained against the seasons, and a roof that let the rain in.

But they didn't see it beneath them. To them, it was a doorway to ministry, a positioning for purpose, a foundation for their future—and mine.

In 1984, they stepped into pastoral ministry. There was no money, no prestige, no earthly appeal in the offer. Still, they said yes. They never questioned whether the circumstances were "worthy" of them. What made them embrace such humble beginnings? It was their assessing opportunity through the lens of divine purpose, not the lens of assumed dignity.

> I've learned this firsthand: Humble people embrace humble things.

There's a principle at work God's kingdom—voluntary abasement often precedes divine elevation. The path to promotion runs through the valley of refining.

Legendary Pentecostal minister and prolific author T.F. Tenney once said, "It is God's job to promote us; it's our job to humble ourselves. If we insist on doing His job, He will do ours."

CHAPTER 3: THE MARK THAT MADE ME

Before we go further, let me offer a caution: Be careful chasing a vision of "significance" or success that is really just a bid for human approval. You may miss God's greatest gifts. He has a peculiar way of packaging them—in wrapping that looks like lack and feels like suffering.

But here's the promise: If you're willing to look beyond the unpolished exterior—if you have the strength of character to see past humble circumstances—you'll often find something remarkable inside. Jesus offers overwhelming joy and lasting fulfillment that no earthly achievement can match.

That trailer behind the church wasn't just a home. It was a lesson in God's economy. Sometimes, our greatest blessings arrive looking like burdens. Our highest callings arrive disguised as low places.

Jesus said, "Learn from me, for I am meek and lowly." The One who formed galaxies chose meekness. He could have summoned angels, yet He walked among the broken.

Romans 12:16 NIV says, "Do not be proud, but be willing to associate with people of low position." That isn't a suggestion—it's a command. And Jesus lived it. He centered His ministry on the hurting, the sinful, the unseen.

The religious elite rejected Him. They would have bowed if He'd come as a conqueror. If He'd wielded power, they'd have submitted. But that wasn't His way.

Instead, He offered humanity a choice: His mark or society's, His humility or the world's pride, His cause or culture's crown, His way or our will.

That same choice remains. Will we chase the marks of worldly success, or carry the imprint of divine humility? Will we define ourselves by society's standards or submit to heaven's scale?

The choice isn't just about what will define us, but whose mark we will carry.

Jesus shows us: True power isn't found in compelling others to submit. It's found in the choice to kneel.

Marks of Rejection

For much of my life, I saw poverty through a personal lens—one shaped by my parents' unwavering commitment to the church. I associated our lack of money with ministry. I believed we were poor *because* of it.

One of my earliest moments as a newly appointed pastor found me seated around a table with church leaders, discussing my commitment to serve this congregation. As I spoke about dedicating my life to their spiritual care, a realization hit me with devastating clarity: God was calling me to serve the very people—and the institution—that had caused some of my deepest childhood wounds.

It was a jolting collision of past and present. I didn't know whether to feel honored or haunted. These faces around the table represented a mixture of great memories and profound hurt. I loved many of them dearly, yet woven through my childhood here was a painful narrative. I had felt different, excluded, and ashamed. We were ridiculed in the community. Our financial struggles were visible. And I traced those struggles back to the church.

Now, in a divine reversal, I was being asked to pour my life into the very place I once saw as the source of my pain. The weight of that calling overwhelmed me, and the tears came before I could stop them. The leaders around the table watched silently, unsure why their new pastor had been suddenly undone by what seemed like a simple ministry meeting.

What they couldn't see was that healing had begun right there in real time. As I wept, something within me was being restored. God was doing soul surgery. By choosing to serve those who had wounded me—without bitterness, without defense—I stepped into the very path that would lead to freedom.

That moment was both deeply humbling and powerfully transformative. I could have let the past be my excuse for withdrawal, cynicism, or a guarded ministry. But instead, God invited me to choose a harder, holier path: the path of humble service. And in that choice, the marks of pain began to transform into marks of grace.

Once that emotional dam broke, there was no stopping the flood. Years of suppressed hurt came rushing out in front of that team. It was awkward. Messy. Raw. But it was real.

What happened? The wounds I had buried in childhood were no longer willing to stay buried. Rejection doesn't go away just because you refuse to look at it. It waits—strengthening, festering—until it finds an opening.

The team sat in stunned silence. They had never seen me this vulnerable. But God was at work, breaking down the wall of pride I had built stone by stone since I was a child. As that wall gave way, I knew I needed to step away—to retreat and meet with the Lord. In that sacred space, He showed me just how deeply rejection had rooted itself in my heart and how pride had grown up around it like a fortress.

The Hidden Wounds

When rejection first wounded me as a child, I did what the flesh always does—I buried it. I pushed it down and kept going. But in His mercy, God chose that moment—right there in leadership—to bring healing through holy brokenness.

He revealed how those early marks of rejection had shaped me. I had sought man's approval over God's glory. I had operated in pride when He was calling me to humility.

As the tears fell, I heard the Spirit whisper 2 Corinthians 12:9: "My grace is sufficient for thee: for my strength is made perfect in weakness."

While the enemy tries to mark us with pride and self-protection, Jesus marks His own with the imprint of humility. That humility is more than a character trait—it's a sign of divine ownership. I am a child of God.

> That was it. God wasn't asking me to lead from strength—but from surrender.

From Wounds to Purpose

I didn't realize God was about to use humility within my wounds—for both my healing and His purpose. The mark of rejection had been carved deep into my soul, and pride had stepped in to mask the pain. Like ancient walls built to keep danger out, pride became my fortress.

But in His wisdom, God used that very mark—the one I thought would destroy me—to shape my calling. Through surrender and grace, what the enemy intended for harm became a testimony of transformation.

I began to see my story through a new lens: one that mirrored Joseph's.

"You intended to harm me, but God intended it all for good. He brought me to this position so I could save the lives of many people" (Genesis 50:20 NLT).

Looking back, I saw Joseph's life with fresh insight. His story was no longer a childhood Bible narrative but a reflection of my own life. Joseph was betrayed by his brothers, falsely accused, imprisoned, and forgotten. I carried my own rejection, convinced the wounds would never heal. These weren't small setbacks. They were defining blows—capable of crushing my purpose, if I let them.

The natural response to pain is protection.

I built emotional strongholds, not knowing they were slowly suffocating me. At the time, I thought I was just guarding my heart. Only later did I understand that those emotional bricks in my wall of safety were made of pride. The thing about pride is that it never heals. Instead, it hides and isolates.

Joseph, too, had a choice. He could have let bitterness take root. He could have used his power in Egypt to retaliate. Instead, he humbled himself and forgave.

That same hard truth met me: Humility—not pride—is the doorway to purpose. My healing began not with achievement or success, but with surrender. With letting God do what pride never could. Then something powerful happened: My scars became tools in His hands.

Joseph saved lives through his pain. I began to minister from mine. My greatest wounds became the very channels through which God now reaches others. What once felt like disqualification became the evidence of my calling.

That's the reversal. Genesis 50:20 isn't just Joseph's story—it's a pattern for every believer who submits to God's refining. It's the promise that He transforms pain into purpose, and wounds into weapons of healing.

Humility didn't just help me survive the mark of rejection—it turned that mark into my ministry.

The spirit of rejection serves as a cruel taskmaster. It speaks in a voice both subtle and savage, whispering lies deep into our souls:

- "You didn't make the cut."

- "You're not good enough."

- "Something's wrong with you."

- "You don't belong here."

- "You'll never measure up."

- "You're not worthy."

Like a bitter wound, each rejection leaves us raw and exposed. To protect ourselves, we build higher walls around our hearts, silently vowing: *Never again. I won't let this happen again.*

But it does happen—again and again. The cycle repeats, each fresh wound reopening old scars. And strangely, those most hurt by rejection often seem to attract more of it, like magnets drawing pain.

It's a wearying cycle—one that we repeat without recognition, redemptive merit, or satisfactory reward. The wounded heart becomes hypersensitive to rejection—seeing it even when it isn't there—while at the same time engaging in behaviors that almost invite it. In trying to avoid pain, we sometimes ensure its return. Life becomes a performance. We fixate on fitting in, being liked, being chosen. We study others like anthropologists, searching for the secret code of acceptance. We begin to believe that to survive, we must either compete with others—or become like them.

That's when the slow death begins.

We perform. We pretend. We perfect our masks. All the while, the need for acceptance infects us like a virus, transforming us from who God created us to be into someone we were never meant to become.

Worse still, rejection releases a kind of spiritual scent that attracts more of the same. Like sharks drawn to blood, those who wound others seem to sense when a soul is already hurting. The enemy sees it too, making the wounded easy prey. With each new blow, old pain resurfaces, and the wound deepens.

The Many Faces of Rejection

If you're reading this with fresh wounds still bleeding, I see you:

- The spouse who feels discarded
- The employee passed over
- The family outcast
- The victim of racism's cruel bite
- The child neglected by those who were meant to nurture

Rejection *will* come. Even Jesus—our perfect Savior—was rejected by His own.

But the wound itself isn't what defines us. It's how we respond that shapes our future. For years, the spirit of rejection shaped the way I saw myself and others. It planted seeds of insecurity so deep that I found myself constantly striving to prove my worth. I worked to elevate myself above others, not realizing I was losing myself in the process.

But Jesus showed me a better way.

Through the valley of brokenness, He taught me that true freedom comes not through recognition, but through surrender. It comes by bowing low.

The day I saw myself through His eyes of love, everything changed. My worth wasn't in performance—it was in my position as His child. Hallelujah!

I learned I could take the lower seat without feeling lesser. My identity was secure in Him.

Now, hear me well—no one makes it through this life without sipping from the bitter cup of rejection. But I feel a word of deliverance rising for someone reading this right now:

If you're bleeding from rejection, hear the word of the Lord—

The same Jesus who was despised and rejected by men, who bore it all at the cross, is reaching out to heal your wounds today.

The Master Potter wants to restore what the enemy tried to destroy in your life.

CHAPTER 3: THE MARK THAT MADE ME

The Lord showed me something powerful: In our frantic quest for acceptance, we aren't really living—we're dying. We sacrifice the identity God breathed into us on the potter's wheel, exchanging authenticity for approval. As we conform to the mold of this world, we suffocate the unique calling God placed in us before we ever took a breath.

Today, when I minister to others carrying the wounds of rejection, I see divine purpose in my journey. Every scar has a story. Every wound carries the potential to become a well of grace. The very mark that once drove me to seek man's approval now compels me to point others to God's perfect love.

So I challenge you, dear reader: Bring your marks before the Lord.

Ask His Spirit to uncover where rejection has written lies across your heart. Let Him reveal where doubt has eclipsed His promises, where fear has silenced your boldness. In His presence, your mark becomes a miracle. Your scar becomes a sermon. Your wound becomes a witness to His redemptive power.

God doesn't waste our wounds. He transforms them into weapons of warfare against the very spirit that inflicted them.

Your mark of rejection—when surrendered—becomes your mark for ministry.

As I now stand in the pulpit once occupied by my father, I marvel at how God redeems. What began as rejection became, in His hands, the signature of my calling. The Lord never promised a life free from markings—only the miraculous transformation of those markings into messages of hope.

Like Jacob, who wrestled with God and walked away with both a limp and a blessing, I carry the scars of a divine encounter. The spirit of rejection that once drove me to build walls of pride has been overthrown by the greater Spirit of adoption, which declares:

"You belong to Me."

Galatians 4:6–7 NLT: "And because we are his children, God has sent the Spirit of his Son into our hearts, prompting us to call out, 'Abba, Father.' Now you are no longer a slave but God's own child. And since you are his child, God has made you his heir."

Discussion Questions for Chapter 3: The Mark That Made Me

Let's Start Here:

Some of God's best work begins in the most unexpected places—trailers, kitchens, garages, borrowed spaces.

What's a time when something meaningful began in a humble or unconventional way?

Maybe it was:

- A business launched from a kitchen table or garage
- A ministry that started in someone's living room
- A hobby or talent developed with duct tape, dollar-store supplies, or YouTube tutorials
- A relationship that blossomed in an unimpressive setting
- A family tradition born out of necessity that became priceless

These stories remind us that God doesn't wait for "perfect" conditions to begin something powerful. Let's celebrate the beauty of small starts that led to big things.

1. Choosing Humble Beginnings

Josh's parents made a home out of a converted trailer behind a church, embracing humble beginnings to follow God's call.

- How can you tell the difference between God leading you into humility and just settling for less?
- Have you ever had to choose between comfort and obedience? What did that look like?

2. Serving the People Who Hurt You

Josh was called to serve the same church that had been the source of his childhood pain.

- Has God ever asked you to love or serve someone who hurt you?
- How can wounds become a place of healing instead of a reason to stay guarded?

3. The Rejection Cycle

This chapter describes how rejection can lead to a pattern of behaviors that unintentionally invite more rejection.

- Why do you think rejection repeats itself so easily?
- What helps someone break out of the cycle of performing for approval?

4. Performing vs. Being Grounded

Josh realized he had spent years building emotional walls and striving to be accepted.

- Where in your life are you tempted to perform or protect rather than live authentically?
- What would it look like to rest in God's approval instead of chasing others' validation?

5. From Rejected to Adopted

Galatians 4:6–7 reminds us that we are not slaves but God's children—heirs through Christ.

- How does remembering you are God's child change how you respond to rejection or criticism?
- What are some ways you can regularly remind yourself of that truth when you feel unseen or unwanted?

Further Reflection:

Pastor Josh wrote, *"God doesn't waste our wounds; He transforms them into weapons of warfare against the spirits that inflict them."*

- How might your painful experiences become tools to minister to others who are walking through something similar?

CHAPTER FOUR:
THE ENEMY OF THE INNER ME

"The heart is deceitful above all things, and desperately wicked; who can know it? I, the Lord, search the heart, I test the mind, even to give every man according to his ways, according to the fruit of his doings."

Jeremiah 17:9–10 NKJV

Pride's most deceptive work is the veil it draws over our eyes, blinding us to ourselves.

Like a slow-growing cataract, it dims our vision until we can no longer see our own reflection. The greatest deception is not in what pride shows us—it's in what pride keeps us from seeing.

The rebellion in heaven, led by Lucifer, is the birthplace of pride. We also see how swiftly God responded, casting down the one who dared to exalt himself. In Isaiah 14:12–15 KJV, we read of the usurper's declarations: "I will ascend into heaven, I will exalt my throne above the stars of God...I will be like the most High." These repeated "I will" statements reveal pride's deadly progression—from self-exaltation to a desire to seize the throne of God.

Lucifer, the covering cherub, was created in perfection. Ezekiel 28:12–15 KJV describes him as "full of wisdom, and perfect in beauty." But that perfection became his downfall. "Thine heart was lifted up because of thy beauty, thou hast corrupted thy wisdom by reason of thy brightness" (Ezekiel 28:17). The very gifts God gave him became the source of his pride.

The consequences were catastrophic. The one who once led heaven's worship was cast down. His fall began in his mind, affected his emotions, and ultimately changed his actions. And a third of heaven's angels followed him—evidence that pride doesn't just destroy; it spreads.

Lucifer's fall is the ultimate warning: If pride could corrupt heaven's most radiant angel in God's presence, how much more should we guard our hearts against its subtle influence? If God did not tolerate pride in heaven, He surely won't tolerate it in His church.

Wherever you are in life, remember this—every time we exalt ourselves, we echo Lucifer's "I will." Every moment of self-glorification carries the seed of rebellion. But God's grace offers a better way: humility. It recognizes that all glory belongs to Him alone. What began in heaven would echo on earth.

Pride's pattern—exaltation followed by expulsion—played out again in the life of King Saul, a man handpicked by God. Once humble, Saul would fall to the same inner enemy: pride.

King Saul's journey from a shy servant hiding among the baggage to a self-absorbed ruler inflated with ambition is one of Scripture's most sobering warnings. When he was first chosen as king, Saul was "little in [his] own eyes" (1 Samuel 15:17 NKJV).

But power and success slowly corrupted his heart.

The turning point came when Saul disobeyed God's command regarding the Amalekites. Rather than utterly destroy what God had condemned, Saul kept the best sheep and oxen—claiming they were for sacrifice. Blinded to his own motives, he justified himself when the prophet Samuel confronted him, rather than repent.

Samuel's words pierced the heart of Saul's disobedience: "To obey is better than sacrifice" (1 Samuel 15:22). That one line tells us much. Obedience flows from what is submitted. Surrender births obedience from the soil of humility, while pride's offspring is always self-justification. A clever disguise for a heart in rebellion.

Humility bows in yielding. Pride builds monuments to its own reasoning. Then came the prophet's next words—still echoing through history: "When you were little in your own eyes... But now... Because you have rejected the word of the Lord, He has also rejected you from being king" (1 Samuel 15:17, 23).

What a tragic shift. The leastness that once qualified Saul for greatness was replaced by self-importance. And that pride disqualified him from God's purpose.

Saul's decline continued—shifting from pride to jealousy of David, slipping into deception, seeking forbidden counsel, and ultimately taking his own life. His tragic end reminds us that pride doesn't just jeopardize our position; it erodes our relationship with God. The very throne Saul fought to protect became the very thing pride caused him to forfeit.

What Moves God

As I look back over my years in ministry, one truth burns deeper with time: God isn't impressed by our platforms, moved by our talents, or swayed by our accomplishments. What captures His heart is a vessel humble enough to carry His presence without trying to claim His glory.

I've watched gifted ministers rise and fall, witnessed thriving ministries crumble, and heard anointed voices go quiet—all because they forgot the source of their effectiveness. They stopped staying small in their own eyes while serving a great God.

Now, every time I step behind a pulpit, I remind myself: It's not about how well I preach. It's about how fully I allow God to take His rightful place as I step back into mine. My decrease makes room for His increase.

Philippians 2:5–11 KJV lays it out plainly:

> **When we forget where God found us, we're in danger of losing where He placed us.**

> *"Let this mind be in you, which was also in Christ Jesus:*
> *Who, being in the form of God, thought it not robbery to be equal with God:*
> *But made himself of no reputation, and took upon him the form of a servant,*
> *and was made in the likeness of men:*
> *And being found in fashion as a man, he humbled himself,*
> *and became obedient unto death, even the death of the cross.*
> *Wherefore God also hath highly exalted him,*
> *and given him a name which is above every name:*
> *That at the name of Jesus every knee should bow,*
> *of things in heaven, and things in earth, and things under the earth;*
> *And that every tongue should confess that Jesus Christ is Lord,*
> *to the glory of God the Father."*

This is the model: not climbing but surrendering. Not claiming status but choosing servanthood. Jesus showed us that the path to glory runs through humility, and the road to exaltation starts with obedience—even when it leads to a cross.

> Then, I discovered something I hadn't expected: Humility invites us to crawl instead of climb.

Let me tell you, that's not the path I went looking for. There's nothing flashy about kneeling when everyone else is racing upward. You won't see it trending. It won't go viral. Bent knees get sore, and strong egos get scraped.

But God showed me something deeper. While I was chasing every rung of success, He was calling me to a different kind of journey. Instead of scaling ladders, He led me through quiet valleys—places of character development, where no one claps and transformation runs deep. It was slower, yes—but that path led me to places that matter. Not always to larger platforms, but always to deeper wells of His presence.

Now I see it clearly: Sometimes the crawl is the climb. Sometimes the slower road is the surer one. And sometimes, the humble route—though it bruises your pride—is the very thing that saves your soul.

Spotting Pride—Even When It Hides

Pride doesn't just live in our words or actions—it hides in our thoughts, shapes our choices, and distorts our view of God, others, and ourselves. It's not content to stay quiet. Pride loves the spotlight. Like a moth to a flame, it rushes toward moments of recognition, drawn to applause, unable to resist the urge to shine. Its compulsive "yes" isn't just about opportunity—it's about fear. Fear of missing out on the glory. Fear of being forgotten.

Scripture makes it plain: "God resists the proud, but gives grace to the humble" (James 4:6 KJV).

We often spot pride right away, don't we? In others, that is. Their swagger, name-dropping, all those credentials hung out like trophies in a glass case, right? There was a time when I'd see it, and I'd make mental notes—quick judgments about the arrogance of others.

But here's the harder truth: That same pride has often crept into my own spirit without me checking it. And when I *do* catch a glimpse of it, it never vanishes. Instead, it whispers. "Look away. You're different. You've earned this." And too often, I've listened.

Eventually, I realized the longest journey wasn't the distance I'd traveled in ministry. It was the few inches between my discerning eye and my honest reflection. That inner shift—from judging others to examining myself—was the beginning of transformation.

Jesus addressed this very issue in Matthew 7:3–5 NKJV:

"And why do you look at the speck in your brother's eye, but do not consider the plank in your own eye? ...First remove the plank from your own eye, and then you will see clearly to remove the speck from your brother's eye."

That may be pride's most dangerous quality—it knows how to stay hidden. Like a blind spot, it obscures our view of ourselves while magnifying everyone else's flaws.

And the nature of deception? You don't know you're deceived.

That's when we receive

> Only when we confront pride's hiding places can humility do its healing work.

grace—the kind that leads to God's embrace and makes room for true connection with His people. Pride rarely walks through the front door. It slips in wearing disguises—some bold, some subtle, all dangerous.

Here are just a few of its common forms:

- **Condemning others while excusing ourselves**—Pride shrinks grace down to a one-way street. We extend it to ourselves while withholding it from others.

- **Fear of failure that fuels perfectionism**—It whispers, *"If I don't get this exactly right, I'm not enough."*

- **Anxiety over others' opinions**—Pride keeps us checking every reaction, fearing disapproval more than disobedience.

- **Worry that masquerades as control**—We mask our mistrust in God's timing by trying to orchestrate every outcome.

- **Hidden resentment and unforgiveness**—Pride refuses to let go because it sees release as weakness, not wisdom.

- **Spiritual superiority**—We measure holiness by how others fall short rather than how Jesus leads us to grow.

- **Resistance to correction**—Pride tells us we're always the teacher, never the student.

- **Comparison and competition**—It pushes us to measure our worth by someone else's success.

Each of these may seem minor—small attitudes, fleeting thoughts. But they grow roots fast. And when they go unchecked, they rob us of grace, strip us of joy, and silence the voice of humility.

The Price of Pride and the Value of Humility

It took years in ministry before I recognized this: Pride and humility both offer something, but their price tags and payouts couldn't be more different.

Pride looks affordable up front. It promises quick rewards—recognition, applause, the thrill of influence. I've chased those things. I've watched others do the same. But pride never shows you the fine print: broken relationships, a dulled sensitivity to the Spirit, and increasing distance from God's presence.

Humility, by contrast, feels expensive. It demands your comfort, your convenience, sometimes even your reputation. It costs you the right to be right. It can keep you hidden when you'd rather be seen. At first glance, it looks like too much to give.

But here's where I miscalculated.

Pride is a cheap counterfeit. It asks little now but takes everything later. Humility may feel costly at first, but it pays out in what truly matters: peace, purpose, protection, and God's favor.

I've witnessed both. I've seen people sprint up self-promotion's ladder only to fall from its highest rung. I've also watched others quietly accept the lowest places—unappealing assignments, dry seasons, unseen tasks—and later be entrusted with greater responsibility and deeper anointing. Their small beginnings produced powerful results. There is no small impact when commitment is steady and faithfulness unwavering. God knows exactly who He can trust to point others to Him.

Pride builds platforms. Humility builds legacy.

The Pride That Masquerades as Humility

"Generosity is giving more than you can, and pride is taking less than you need."—Khalil Gibran[v]

There's a sacred rhythm between giving and receiving—a divine flow that pride often disrupts. Generous hearts give beyond reason because they trust in God's supernatural provision. Humble hearts receive without shame because they know dependence is not weakness; it's design.

The person marked by true humility can both give sacrificially and receive gratefully. Their confidence isn't in their own sufficiency but in God's endless supply—whether He provides directly or through the kindness of others.

Gibran's quote challenges us to examine our motivations. Are we giving because we trust God, or withholding because we trust only ourselves? Are we refusing help because we truly have enough, or because we're afraid to appear needy?

Scarcity fear whispers: "There's not enough. Protect what's yours. Save for the crisis." That fear convinces us to measure, ration, and withhold—whether it's money, time, energy, or even love. And while it may sound wise, it's often pride disguised. Pride that refuses to rely on anyone else—even God—for provision. So, instead of asking for what we need, we "take less" and wear it like humility.

But it isn't humility. It's self-protection. It's pride operating in reverse.

I've seen this often in ministry: people who quietly develop what I call a *scarcity martyr complex*. They pride themselves on needing little, asking for nothing, and accepting less. On the surface, it looks noble—until you realize the focus isn't actually on God or others. It's still on self.

---

v Khalil Gibran, *Sand and Foam* (New York: Alfred A. Knopf, 1926), quoted in Goodreads, https://www.goodreads.com/quotes/45514-generosity-is-giving-more-than-you-can-and-pride-is.

In contrast, real humility can say, "I need help," with the same grace it says, "I'd love to help." It accepts provision with worship, knowing all good things come from above. It trusts that we live not by calculation, but by abundance.

Because that's the truth: In God's kingdom, generosity multiplies. The more we give, the more we find we have. The more we receive with open hands, the more we're able to share. There's no scarcity in the hands of a faithful God.

The Divine Protection

Sometimes, God lets us lose—not to punish us, but to protect us.

Pride makes success dangerous. It convinces us we earned it, that we're owed more, that we can manage the blessing without the Giver. But humility creates a safe place for success to land. It opens the heart to God's grace and closes the door to self-glory.

I've admired the visible outcomes of growth, gifting, and influence but have learned that without the hidden strength of surrender there's nothing to sustain the performance. Without a foundation laid by God, the risk of becoming all shine and no substance is high. The outer structure might look impressive, but it's hollow at the core.

I've learned that not every loss was the enemy's attack. Some were God's mercy in disguise.

The very thing I begged God to preserve, He sometimes allowed to fall apart—not to harm me, but to humble me. To teach me that I'm safest when surrendered. That success without surrender is a setup for spiritual collapse.

> Humility doesn't grow in comfort—it's forged in challenge.

God doesn't just want to anoint us. He wants to protect us from ourselves. And humility is His covering.

When Jesus says, "Learn of me, for I am meek and lowly in heart" (Matthew 11:29), He is not suggesting humility be a fallback or occasional virtue. He's inviting us to adopt it as our defining posture. That transformation becomes instinctive to how we think, respond, and lead—but not without testing. And these tests don't come with warning signs or scheduled dates. They show up in real time, through real pain, with real consequences.

They arrive disguised—as rejection, correction, failure, or fear. Through them, God chisels our character, strips our pride, and builds something deeper than public success. These four tests have shaped me more than any platform ever could.

Humility's Testing Ground:

1. Rejection's Sting

I never expected rejection to be one of humility's greatest teachers. Doors I thought God had opened slammed shut. People I had invested in walked away. Opportunities I felt sure about disappeared without explanation. Each time, I was left exposed and disappointed.

But rejection stripped away what I thought I needed and revealed what I truly relied on. I learned that humility doesn't demand to be seen or accepted—it stays faithful even when overlooked. Those moments taught me to root my worth not in applause but in God's unwavering love.

2. Criticism's Bite

Few things cut as sharply as critique. Early in ministry, every criticism felt like a threat. I either bristled with defensiveness or collapsed in insecurity.

But humility taught me to hear differently. It gave me the strength to listen without reacting, to ask, "Is there truth in this?" even when it stung. Not all critics were right—but some were sent. And humility allowed me to grow instead of resist.

3. Condemnation's Weight

The heaviest blows didn't come from others—they came from within. Times when I failed, when I missed the mark, when my words didn't line up with my walk—those moments carried a crushing sense of unworthiness.

Humility didn't ignore my shortcomings; it brought them to the cross. It helped me own them without being owned by them. That grace became the pathway to healing and growth.

Psalm 26:2 NKJV: "Examine me, O Lord, and prove me; try my mind and my heart."

4. Fear's Grip

Fear and humility seem unrelated—but they are deeply connected. Fear of failing. Fear of not measuring up. Fear of being exposed. I often called it humility, but it was pride in disguise—afraid of being seen as weak or unworthy.

When I stopped hiding behind spiritual phrases and admitted my fears, I found freedom.

> **True humility doesn't mask fear—it faces it.**

> **God wasn't looking for strength; He was waiting for surrender.**

Those tests did more than humble me—they exposed the fault lines beneath my identity. I began to see how much of my striving came from fear of being unseen, unheard, or unworthy. Pride isn't always loud. Sometimes, it hides behind performance, behind false humility, behind the fear of disappearing. I had to confront the lies I'd unknowingly believed: that submission made me smaller, that humility meant losing myself. But in reality, surrender was the doorway to discovering who I truly was in Christ.

They suggest humility is weakness—a loss of identity rather than the discovery of it.

But none of that is true.

In the upside-down nature of God's kingdom, submission doesn't strip us of identity—it secures it. Humility doesn't make us smaller—it reveals who we truly are. When we stop chasing recognition and start surrendering to God's purpose, we don't vanish. We actually become.

The world insists we should build our brand, make our mark, and take up space. But Jesus calls us to something deeper: Take up your cross. And in that lowering, we rise. In that surrender, we gain strength. Humility becomes the posture where our truest, God-given identity is not only protected—but fully realized.

There's a war within each of us—a constant tension between who we used to be and who God is shaping us to become. Pride isn't just a bad habit; it's our default setting. It reacts before we even think. It's that first, instinctive surge that rises to defend, impress, or assert.

I remember one Sunday when someone openly challenged something I had just preached. Before my mind had a chance to reason, my flesh was already armed—defensive words loaded, posture stiffened, heart racing to protect itself. That's how quickly the old nature moves—fast, reactive, and often wrong.

Neuroscience research shows that our emotional brain (the amygdala) often reacts before our rational brain (the prefrontal cortex), which explains why our initial responses to pride, fear, or anger can feel so overwhelming.[vi] No wonder Scripture tells us to be "slow to speak, slow to wrath" (James 1:19).

That day became a mirror. I didn't respond perfectly. But by the grace of God, a second thought came—quieter, humbler. It nudged me with questions like, "What if there's truth in their words?" and "What if this is a moment to reflect Christ, not defend yourself?"

That's the grace of second nature.

Our first instincts are loud and automatic. They're shaped by past wounds, flesh patterns, and unrenewed thinking. But our second nature—the one born of the Spirit—reminds us who we are in Christ. It gives us a holy pause to choose a better response.

It's a daily battle. Sometimes I catch myself mid-sentence or mid-reaction, realizing it's the old nature trying to take the wheel. But the longer I walk with God, the more familiar that second nature becomes—not just as a correction, but as a calling.

That's the reality of being born again. It's not a behavior upgrade—it's a

> **We aren't just people trying to act better. We are people who have been made new.**

---

vi Daniel Goleman, *Emotional Intelligence: Why It Can Matter More Than IQ* (New York: Bantam Books, 1995).

complete identity transformation. The old nature doesn't get polished; it gets crucified.

But just because we've been given a new nature doesn't mean the old one goes quietly. Pride doesn't surrender without a fight. It lurks in the corners of our instincts, waiting for us to react rather than reflect. That's why we have to walk in the Spirit, not just talk about the Spirit.

I used to think humility was about thinking less of myself. But that's not it. Humility is about thinking rightly of myself—seeing myself as God sees me. No more, no less. It's standing in the truth of who I am in Him: chosen, loved, and secure enough not to have to prove anything to anyone.

When I walk in that reality, I don't need to dominate a room to feel important. I don't need the last word to feel validated. I don't need the spotlight to feel seen. Being born again means I've already been approved by the only One whose opinion matters.

Learning to actively be still doesn't come naturally—especially when so much of our identity used to be wrapped in motion. Filling every silence, owning every room, chasing every opportunity felt necessary. But humility doesn't strive to be everywhere or say everything. It learns to trust that God's affirmation is enough. And that kind of trust creates space—for stillness, for reflection, for the Spirit to speak before we do.

Pride moves fast. It rushes to defend, to justify, to prove. But humility slows the moment down. It gives space to listen, to reflect, to respond with grace instead of ego.

Learning to Pause

I've learned the value of what I now call a holy pause. It's the intentional moment I take between my first instinct and my next action. It's the deep breath before I speak. The prayer before I react. The silence before I explain myself. In that pause, the Spirit often whispers something different than my flesh was shouting. Choosing submission is not without regenerative rewards. This isn't weakness. It's strength under control. It's self-

> **Transformation happens in that space between reaction and response.**

awareness steeped in surrender. And more often than not, it keeps me from saying or doing something I'll regret later.

Humility isn't just a trait. It's a practice. And the more I pause, the more I live from my new nature—anchored, secure, and shaped by grace.

The Born-Again Reality

I'm still unraveling the layers of this truth: Pride may be our first nature, it's no longer our true nature. Through salvation and sanctification, God has given us a new nature.

While pride may be our first instinct, it shouldn't take the prime spot in our interactions. In Christ, we're learning to see ourselves, and others, through the lens of grace. Every day presents multiple opportunities to choose between these two natures: when someone receives the recognition we think we deserve, when our ideas are overlooked, and when our ministry seems small compared to others, pride springs up first, but humility can win if we choose.

Watching this second nature become more ingrained has been one of the most beautiful parts of my spiritual journey. Yes, pride still shows up first most of the time, but its voice grows weaker as humility's grows stronger. What once felt like a constant battle slowly became a new way of being.

Looking back over years in ministry, I see how God has patiently worked to make humility more instinctive. While pride still attempts its first strike, the Holy Ghost has developed a quicker recognition and response. Second nature is becoming first, and that old nature is showing up less frequently.

We're all on this journey of learning to let our new nature in

> Remember: While pride may try to be first in line, humility carries the authority of Heaven.

Christ overcome our Adamic one. It is not about perfection. It's about progression—resisting pride's pull and learning to choose humility's path with consistency.

And in God's kingdom, the last shall be first.

Samson's Fall: A Cautionary Tale of Lost Consecration

Let me share this sobering truth about Samson's tragic fall. Though he was chosen as a Nazarite from birth, set apart by divine purpose, his pride became the cause of his destruction.

What a warning this holds for us! Consider this mighty man of God, who could tear lions apart with his bare hands. Yet, it was not the Philistines who ultimately defeated him; his pride brought him low. Samson saw his strength as his possession rather than God's power flowing through a yielded vessel.

Proverbs 16:5 KJV states, "Everyone that is proud in heart is an abomination to the Lord, though hand join in hand, he shall not be unpunished."

Pride carries a terrible price tag. You can join hands with every powerful ally, but you cannot escape pride's consequences. When we take credit for what God's power has accomplished, we walk the same dangerous path as Samson. He forgot that his strength lay not in his hair but in his covenant, not in his ability but in his consecration to God.

Let Samson's fall be our warning: Pride is not just another struggle—it is an abomination to the Lord. When we exalt ourselves instead of recognizing His power working through us, we set ourselves up for a fall. Pride's payment plan never fails to collect what is due.

> Oh, how careful we must be, even in our holiest consecrations, that pride doesn't creep in and poison our sacrifice.

There is no room for self-exaltation when we set ourselves apart in order to draw closer to God. Even in our most sacred commitments, that snare of pride whispers, "Look how spiritual you are. See how much more consecrated you are than others?"

The moment we begin feeling superior because of our consecration, we have corrupted its purpose. When we begin thinking, "I'm better than my brother or sister because of my sacrifice," we've turned our holy offering into an unholy boast. True sanctification does not allow for comparison. Setting ourselves apart for God is about Him, not about us appearing more righteous than others. The moment pride enters consecration, its power is broken. Remember—every vow, fast, and act of devotion must be wrapped in humility.

Wheat and Tares: A Picture of True Humility

As the Reverend T. F. Tenney once put it, "Humility is the most sensitive of all graces. The moment you think you have it, it's gone."[vii]

I felt the Holy Ghost illuminate something profound to me regarding the parable of the wheat and tares. There's a guiding principle in nature that reflects true submission.

Consider the wheat field at harvest time. As the head of wheat grows fuller with precious grain, it bows lower toward the earth. Its fruitfulness is reflected in its posture; the fuller it grows, the lower it bows. What a vivid picture of genuine spiritual maturity—strength revealed through surrender.

Now let's examine the nature of a tare. The Bible's reference to a "tare" points to a specific weed known as *darnel*, also called false wheat or cockle.

Key characteristics of tares:

1. They look almost identical to wheat in early growth.

2. Their roots often intertwine with those of the wheat.

3. They are poisonous to humans if consumed.

4. They can only be definitively distinguished once the grain heads appear.

This is the insight of the parable: tares look so similar to wheat that separating them too soon risks damaging the good grain. That's why the master says to wait until harvest.

At harvest time, tares stand tall and proud, their heads lifted high. Why? Because they bear no fruit. They are all show and no substance—height without harvest.

The more God fills you with His gifts, wisdom, and anointing, the more your flesh and spirit will wrestle over whether to bow in humility or stand in pride. Just as the fullest wheat bends low, those who carry

---

vii T. F. Tenney, "Humility in Leadership," Apostolic Information Service, November 1, 2012, https://www.apostolic.edu/humility-in-leadership-entire-article/.

the most spiritual fruit walk in true humility. They willingly lower themselves under God's mighty hand, recognizing Jesus as the source of every good thing.

> **When someone stands tall in pride, refusing to bow, it's often because they bear no fruit.**

But those bearing kingdom fruit—reaching souls with the Gospel, restoring families, changing lives—are found on their knees, giving all glory to God.

Which are you? Standing tall like a tare in pride, or bowing low like ripe wheat, heavy with fruit? Remember, it's not the height of your posture but the weight of your fruit that reveals your authenticity in God's harvest field.

We must allow the Spirit to search our motives daily. For in heaven's eyes, it's not just what we do that matters, but why we do it. The heart behind every act of service determines whether we are sowing wheat—or tares—in the field of God.

Discussion Questions for Chapter 4: "The Enemy of the Inner Me"

Let's Start Here:

Sometimes the person in the mirror needs the advice we're giving to everyone else.

Can you think of a time when you dished out wisdom you weren't exactly living out yourself?

Maybe it was:

- Telling someone to stay calm while you were stressed to the max

- Advising healthy habits with fast food in hand

- Encouraging organization while drowning in your own clutter

- Urging someone to ignore opinions while secretly spiraling over them

- Giving relationship advice while your own was on the struggle bus

We've all had those "Do as I say, not as I do" moments. Let's laugh a little—and learn a lot—as we grow in self-awareness and humility.

1. Pride's Blind Spot

The chapter highlights how pride often blinds us to our own motives, even as we clearly spot it in others.

- Why do you think it's easier to notice pride in someone else than to recognize it in yourself?

- Can you recall a time when someone helped you see something in your heart that you hadn't noticed?

2. The Split-Second Battle

Josh describes the tension between our first reaction (usually shaped by pride or fear) and our second, Spirit-led response. He's learning to take what he calls a "holy pause" in that space between.

- What does this internal tension look like for you?
- What helps you slow down in the moment so pride doesn't take the lead?

3. Wheat vs. Weeds

The illustration about real wheat bowing down when it's full—and weeds standing tall without substance—reminds us that humility and maturity go hand in hand.

- How can you tell when your confidence is rooted in God versus propped up by pride?
- What does it look like to walk humbly while still using your gifts with boldness?

4. False Humility, Hidden Pride

Sometimes we refuse help not out of humility but because we're too proud to appear weak.

- Have you ever said no to something good because you didn't want to seem vulnerable?
- How can you tell the difference between genuine humility and protecting your image?

5. The Tests That Shape Us

The chapter outlines four ways God tests and shapes our humility: rejection, correction, failure, and fear.

- Which of these have been the most challenging for you?
- What has God revealed about your heart through those tests?

Further Reflection

King Saul forgot that he started in a place of smallness. Samson forgot where his strength came from. Both lost their way when pride crept in.

- What helps you stay grounded and grateful for what God has done in your life?

- How can you practice humility when everything seems to be going well?

CHAPTER 5: THE COMPETITIVE PRISON OF PRIDE

"Let another man praise you, and not your own mouth;
a stranger, and not your own lips."

Proverbs 27:2 NKJV

When I was nine years old, our small school basketball team made it to the regional championship. The odds were stacked against us—the referee was the father of one of our opponents' star players. As expected, I fouled out under questionable calls, and without me, our team unraveled. We lost, convinced the game had been stolen through bias.

I didn't have a hoop or a ball at home. I had no training, no private coaching—just a strange ability that felt beyond me. Looking back, I played with what I now recognize as raw anointing—gift without refinement. What stayed with me wasn't just the loss, but the weight of knowing I had something special and still couldn't win.

It planted in me a quiet belief—that injustice could overpower anointing—even if my nine-year-old mind didn't call it that. It just felt like a blow to the core of who I was.

After the game, something unforgettable happened. The tournament organizers called me to the stage to receive the Athletic Award, and the gym erupted in applause. Spectators stood, cheering with the kind of affirmation that silences doubt. Even biased officiating couldn't deny what everyone had seen.

Trophy in hand, I slipped to the back of the gym. That's when a stranger approached me. I still don't know who he was or why he was there. He moved with quiet purpose, placed his hand on my shoulder, and said words that would echo through my life:

"Son, you must learn humility."

I remember stiffening with indignation. *I already know that!* I thought. *Why are you telling me this?* But those words branded my heart. Now, decades later, I see what he was really saying: Favor without humility turns into entitlement. God had sent a messenger— perhaps even an angel—to plant

Favor without humility turns into entitlement.

a seed I wouldn't fully understand until years later.

Favor may open doors, but only humility keeps them from slamming shut.

The gifts of God are freely given, not earned. I didn't have a hoop in my driveway, and my gift wasn't really basketball—it was the ability to do things I shouldn't have been able to do. It was God.

"For God's gifts and His call can never be withdrawn" (Romans 11:29 NLT).

God doesn't revoke His gifts or change His mind. His spiritual gifts—like teaching, healing, or prophecy—are permanent endowments. His calling remains intact, even when we falter or fail. His character doesn't shift with our performance; He gives out of His will, not based on our worth.

But pride is the enemy's sabotage tool. It latches on to those gifts and whispers a dangerous lie: *This is about you.* It creeps in right where our anointing shines brightest. And if we aren't watchful, the very thing God gave us to glorify Him becomes a stage for self-glory.

I've seen it again and again: When supernatural ability flows through ordinary people, two paths appear. The first is wide and seductive. It tells you that you're different, exceptional—that you've earned the right to operate beyond the norm. The second is narrow, quiet, and requires constant awareness. It reminds you that your gifts are not proof of personal greatness—they're evidence of a great God choosing to work through you.

That stranger in the gym knew something I didn't: Anointing draws attention, and attention, if we're not careful, breeds the deadliest poison to divine purpose—the belief that we deserve the spotlight. But our gifts don't prove *we're* amazing. They prove *God* is.

One of the most sobering lessons I've learned is this: The very gifts God gives us to glorify Him can start pointing back to us if we lose sight of humility. Pride doesn't just come before a fall—it all but guarantees that what God once freely gave will be redirected if it no longer serves His purpose. God won't let His glory be hijacked. When ego grows, perspective shrinks. Instead of reflecting the Giver, we begin promoting ourselves.

I didn't see that at first. I thought my gift was a sign I had arrived, confirmation that I was special and capable. But over time, I discovered the real test wasn't whether I *had* a gift—it was how I handled the attention it brought. The more I exalted myself, the more the spotlight burned rather than revealed. The more I claimed the stage, the more distant God's presence.

Eventually, I had to admit something difficult: I wasn't just climbing the wrong ladder—I was climbing it for the wrong reason. My motives were fueled by insecurity and pride. I needed to be the best. The most anointed. The most admired. I confused that hunger for calling, but it was actually captivity.

Back then, someone else's win felt like my loss. I saw every success around me as a threat and every opportunity as a competition. I minimized others' achievements, amplified their flaws, and even when I offered compliments, they were tinged with quiet superiority. I couldn't celebrate without comparing. I couldn't affirm without measuring. But in trying to be bigger, I was shrinking—and the people I hurt most weren't strangers. They were the very ones I loved.

Opening up about my struggles, shortcomings, and missteps hasn't been about appearing transparent—it's been about becoming vulnerable enough to say, "I'm still learning. I don't have it all figured out. I need help too." That's not weakness; it's the beginning of strength.

Honest reflection started with some painful but necessary questions: *Who am I when no one's watching? Do I make people feel heard, or do I talk over them? Do I listen, or do I only wait to speak?* These weren't just exercises in self-awareness. They were moments of divine confrontation—mirrors God used to show me the condition of my spirit.

For most of my life, I didn't just want to win—I *had* to. Every setting became a competition, every interaction a silent scoreboard. If someone else succeeded, it felt like a loss for me. I minimized other people's achievements, pointed out their flaws, and masked jealousy as concern.

My own worth was tangled up in being "the best," and anyone else's shine felt like a threat to mine.

I told myself it was excellence, but it was really pride in disguise. The twist? While I believed I was outpacing everyone else, I was isolating myself. I wasn't just hurting others—I was locking myself inside a prison of comparison and competition. The first step out was vulnerability.

My story was marked by an insatiable hunger to be first. What I saw as drive and excellence, the Lord later revealed as bondage. Every opportunity became a battleground where anything less than first place felt like failure. Competitiveness pulsed through me like fire—but it was a counterfeit flame. I needed to be the most anointed, the most admired, the most in demand. The top of every mountain had to bear my name. What I thought was ambition turned out to be a golden chain—shiny, but suffocating. I mistook it for a crown, not realizing it was crushing the very spirit God was trying to shape. I couldn't see the truth that would eventually undo me: "the first shall be last, and the last shall be first" (Matthew 19:30 KJV).

Scripture offers a sobering truth: "God resists the proud, but gives grace to the humble" (James 4:6 KJV). When our souls are restless, God's favor feels far away, and something seems unsettled within, pride may be the silent culprit. The road to freedom begins with recognition. We can't break free from what we won't name. But when we acknowledge pride's presence, we disarm its power.

If you can name it, you can tame it.

The moment I clearly identified what was stirring in my spirit—whether pride masquerading as confidence or fear posing as caution—I

> There's something transformative about bringing hidden struggles into the light of honest recognition.

began to regain authority over what once controlled me. Pride thrives in vagueness, in the unnamed shadows of our emotional world. But clarity disrupts its grip. When we can name what we're truly feeling, we begin to reclaim power and walk in freedom.

Pride is cunning in its defenses. One of its most subtle tactics is convincing us to minimize our flaws and ignore our deficiencies. We avoid honest self-examination because facing our inadequacies feels threatening. Pride builds a shield—a protective barrier that keeps us from acknowledging weakness, exploring fear, confronting failure, or naming our wounds. While this shield may temporarily protect our ego, it ultimately blocks the growth and healing we most need.

At one point, the Lord began prompting me to pay attention to my spirit after certain interactions—leaving family gatherings, ministry meetings, or business conversations. Did those moments stir fresh hurt or expose something festering within me? The Holy Ghost revealed that when my emotional reactions were outsized or disproportionate, it often pointed to pride occupying a deeper place in my heart. Our relationships—especially within the body of Christ—can reflect more about our inner spiritual condition than we realize.

My friend A. J. Holloway, a Greek scholar, once shared a truth that changed how I see Scripture: the "sword of the Spirit" (Ephesians 6:17) can also be translated as "surgical knife." That revelation shifted everything for me. The Word of God isn't meant to slice others down in arguments or serve as a blunt weapon to prove a point. It is meant to cut with precision—to perform deep, internal work as a tool of self-examination, transformation, and refinement. Scripture is God's surgical instrument, not ours.

When we truly enter His presence, something holy happens. Pride cannot stand in the atmosphere of His glory. No one emerges from genuine time with God still clinging to self-exaltation. Before His throne, all accomplishments fade and our self-importance dissolves. That shift transforms us from self-appointed surgeons—quick to wield verses to correct others—into humble patients, willing to be cut open so healing can begin.

For years, I believe God had been trying to teach me this truth. But sometimes it takes running into the wall of exhaustion to finally recognize the futility of constant striving. I hit that wall when I realized I was sprinting on a success treadmill—always moving but going nowhere. It was endless effort with no eternal direction. That's when I surrendered.

That's when I stopped using Scripture to fix others and let it finally cut me.

There's a holy shift that happens when we stop saying, "I'm the victim," and begin saying, "I'm the patient." In the healing hands of the Great Physician, pain takes on new purpose. Instead of circling the same wounds, we let the discomfort drive us forward. We begin to trust that God will use even our suffering as fuel for healing, growth, and grace.

I don't write these words from a pedestal. I write from the recovery room. I'm not offering theories—I'm offering lived experience. Like someone in remission from a long illness, I simply want to share the path that's led me closer to wholeness. Not because I've arrived, but because I'm still walking.

Pride always craves more: more applause, more achievement, more attention. But it stands on shaky ground—the unstable foundation of flesh-driven identity. You can't satisfy something that's always reaching. True spiritual health requires frequent heart checks. Is this decision driven by love or ego? Would Jesus lead this way? Are my motives pure, or is pride sneaking in under ambition's disguise?

These answers rarely come in meetings or metrics. They rise in the stillness—on the floor of the prayer room, in the whisper of conviction, in the quiet yielding of self to Spirit.

Sometimes, God protects the ministry or the work we're building, not because we're flawless—but because He's merciful. He loves the people we serve too much to let our pride wreck what they need. He might let the project stand while gently confronting the builder. We're not where we are because of brilliance or gifting—we're here because God allowed it, often in spite of ourselves. And when He starts reshaping the heart, everything else begins to change too.

Over time, God began to shift something deep inside me. The inner posture that once defaulted to competition began learning how to celebrate others. The instinct to criticize softened into a voice of encouragement. Condescension gave way to genuine appreciation. Where I once measured myself against others, I started to connect with them instead.

Today, I rejoice when others succeed. I see God's favor on their lives and value them for who they are—not as benchmarks to compare myself against, but as fellow travelers on the journey. That shift didn't come through willpower or self-improvement. It came through surrender. It came through the Spirit's slow, faithful transformation. And He used someone closest to me. My wife.

One day, Keesha said something that should have awakened me: "I can't tell you anything negative about yourself." I should have heard her heart. Instead, my pride took offense. I made myself the wounded one in a moment where she was offering me truth in love. That's the strange twist of pride—it wounds us when we're told we've wounded someone else.

When God finally revealed me to myself, the fortress I had built began to crack. The image I'd worked so hard to preserve—strong, confident, unshakable—started to unravel. I was a man who once viewed tears as weakness, now weeping in front of my wife. Pride had convinced me that vulnerability was something to avoid. Humility was now showing me it was the very path to healing.

That revelation sparked a wave of repentance. One by one, I began making things right. I apologized to my children, who had grown up with a father who always had to win the conversation. I apologized to my siblings, who had carried the weight of my constant competition. I apologized to the congregation I served, who had endured a leader more committed to being right than being kind. I apologized to every person who had been cut by the sharp edges of my unchecked ambition.

My relentless drive to win had cost me more than I realized— especially in the currency of relationships. In chasing victories, I lost the hearts of those closest to me. They didn't pull away because they stopped caring; they pulled away because pride had made real connection impossible. But transparency led me to an unexpected truth: People weren't waiting to criticize me—they were waiting to connect.

My pride had erected walls between us, and only true repentance could tear them down. Each confession, each honest conversation, each act of humility removed a brick. Slowly, the walls began to fall.

Pride didn't vanish. As long as I'm breathing, it never will. But awareness became the conduit of repair and restructure. Now, when pride rises, I try to name it in real time—with a quiet "I'm sorry, I shouldn't have said that," or a humbling "That was pride speaking—

please forgive me." Conviction within a softened heart speaks clearer than it once did: "I was wrong to respond that way."

This battle hasn't ended. It's still flesh against Spirit, carnality against surrender. Pride loosens it grip with excruciating slowness. Daily monitoring is necessary. But every small victory—each honest admission or heartfelt apology—has rebuilt relationships that pride once threatened to destroy.

God, like a wise physician, didn't just treat my symptoms. He helped me see the deeper pattern. These weren't one-off moments to manage—they were signals of something buried: a root system that needed to be uncovered and removed.

Henry David Thoreau wrote, "There are a thousand hacking at the branches of evil to one who is striking at the root."[viii] The same holds true with pride. Most of us stay busy managing its symptoms—sharp words, competitive impulses, a need to win, constant comparison, and critical attitudes. All the "leaves." But like a gardener who only trims what's above the surface, we end up fighting the same battles over and over. The cycle doesn't stop until we get beneath the behaviors and deal with what's actually feeding them.

Then came a surprising discovery: Pride wears two faces. We often recognize it in bold forms—swagger, boasting, self-importance. But pride also has a quieter, shadowed side that's harder to detect. It can show up as overconfidence—insisting on being right, refusing to admit mistakes, dismissing others' input, or assuming superiority. Or it can emerge as insecurity—constant self-doubt, fear of judgment, craving validation, and living in a loop of comparison.

What intrigued me was how both extremes—confidence that overreaches and insecurity that undercuts—stemmed from the same root: pride. They look different, but they're both centered on self. They both drain our mental and emotional reserves, distort how we relate to others, resist the grace of God, and block spiritual growth. The real issue isn't how we see ourselves—it's that we're fixated on ourselves. Whether inflated or deflated, self-focus is still self-focus. If we want freedom, we must shift our attention from earthly applause to heavenly approval. The

---

viii Henry David Thoreau, *Walden; or, Life in the Woods* (Boston: Ticknor and Fields, 1854), 75.

> **When we align our vision with the truth of Scripture, our weakness doesn't disqualify us—it becomes the doorway to His strength.**

Word of God, not the changing opinions of the crowd, must become our mirror.

As Paul declared in 2 Corinthians 12:9–10, God's grace shines brightest in our frailty: "My grace is sufficient for thee: for my strength is made perfect in weakness. Most gladly therefore will I rather glory in my infirmities, that the power of Christ may rest upon me. Therefore I take pleasure in infirmities...for when I am weak, then am I strong."

This divine exchange turns what we try to hide into what God chooses to use. Our emptiness makes room for His power.

The most perilous moment in our spiritual walk is not when we're struggling with pride—but when we think we've conquered it. Scripture warns, "Let him that thinketh he standeth take heed lest he fall" (1 Corinthians 10:12 KJV). Pride is never far from the surface. It hides, waiting for the right conditions: a cutting remark, a moment of correction, an old wound reopened. Just when we think we've matured past it, it reappears—subtle but strong—reminding us that the battle isn't over. Pride doesn't just want a moment of recognition; it wants residency in the heart.

The Christian life carries a tension we must learn to live with: Sin is no longer our identity, yet it still lingers as an unwelcome companion. Though we are redeemed, the presence of our old nature demands continual surrender. "Die daily" isn't just a biblical command—it's a spiritual necessity. Every morning presents a fresh choice: to go low instead of climbing high, to serve instead of dominating, to crucify self rather than protect pride. These daily decisions lead us back to the cross, where true exaltation is born from deliberate humility.

There's a widely circulated story, often attributed to Cherokee tradition but of uncertain origin, that captures the essence of our internal conflict. A grandfather tells his grandson about two wolves locked in battle inside every person. One wolf is evil driven by pride, envy, greed, and arrogance. The other is good marked by peace, humility, kindness, and faith. When the boy asks which wolf wins, the elder responds, "The one you feed."

That simple truth holds weight. We all face a daily struggle between flesh and spirit, pride and humility. It's not a onetime decision but an ongoing war—a tug-of-war between the desire for prominence and the call to surrender. Humility is the crown the world forgets. It doesn't shout or demand attention, yet it holds more power than the loudest self-promotion. While culture urges us to rise, influence, and impress, the way of Jesus calls us to descend—to take the low road that leads to true greatness.

When praise comes, we can point it back to God. When offense tries to provoke us, we can respond with gentleness instead of retaliation. When success calls, we can remember

> **Every day brings fresh opportunities to choose humility.**

who gave us the ability. And when leadership is placed in our hands, we can use it to serve rather than dominate. These aren't natural reactions—but each humble choice trains our spirit and shapes our character to mirror Christ more fully.

We tend to associate pride with overt superiority—boasting, posturing, and the urge to outshine. But pride can be far more subtle. Sometimes it hides in our frantic efforts to prove we're just as good as everyone else. That quiet desperation to stay equal, to not fall behind, to match the standard others have set—it's still pride, only dressed in insecurity.

Philippians 2:7 says Jesus "made himself of no reputation, and took upon him the form of a servant." That single verse is a breathtaking window into the humility of Christ. The King of Glory—who created the universe and commands angel armies—voluntarily set aside His divine privileges. He didn't just act like a servant. He became one.

That truth pierced me deeply. While I was busy clinging to status, defending positions, and striving to be seen, Jesus had chosen the lowest seat. The Savior who rightfully deserved all honor lived as a carpenter's son. The One who could have summoned heaven's armies instead chose to kneel with a towel and wash the feet of broken men.

The Holy Ghost confronted my motives: If Jesus—God in flesh—laid down His reputation, why was I so desperate to preserve mine? That conviction exposed a painful truth. I had been more concerned with building my name than advancing His kingdom.

God began reshaping my vision of greatness. True elevation doesn't come from climbing—it comes from descending. It's not about being known; it's about making Him known. Jesus didn't just preach humility—He lived it, died with it, and rose in glory because of it.

That challenge from God to take a look at myself with His perspective shifted everything. Every title became a tool for service. Every platform became an altar of surrender. Following Jesus meant making myself of no reputation, carrying my cross daily, and choosing the basin and towel over applause and attention.

True transformation doesn't happen by accident. It requires a deliberate process—one that moves us from awareness to action. That journey begins with **education**. We must learn to recognize pride's subtle disguises, understand the depth of humility's power, examine the ripple effects of our behavior, and glean wisdom from those who've walked the road before us.

Next comes **evaluation**. Honest reflection on our relationships, business habits, and reactions to criticism can uncover hidden motives and unmet needs. We must ask hard questions: Am I doing this for God's glory or for my own recognition? Is this response coming from humility—or insecurity?

Then comes **elimination**. Growth requires that we strip away what no longer serves God's purpose: destructive behaviors, toxic thought patterns, false identities, and the many manifestations of pride that sabotage our progress.

And finally, **equipping**. As God removes what doesn't belong, He also builds something new—healthier response patterns, deeper emotional intelligence, stronger communication, and the kind of relational strength that only humility can sustain.

Pride is a master of distortion. One of its most dangerous effects is how it clouds our vision. When ego inflates, clarity deflates. Case in point:

I was preparing for a podcast interview about this very book on humility when I faced a telling decision: choose between two pairs of glasses. The older ones framed my face better, but I couldn't read my notes. The newer ones gave me sharp vision but, in my mind, weren't as flattering.

It struck me—this wasn't just a wardrobe dilemma. It was a metaphor. Pride wants us to look good, even if it costs us the ability to see clearly. It craves perception over insight, appearance over substance. But humility chooses clarity. It prioritizes what helps us perceive rightly, even if it means letting go of what flatters us most. That small moment revealed a much larger truth about the internal battle between how we appear and who we're becoming.

Once we recognize that clarity is more valuable than appearance, it challenges us to reevaluate the choices we've made—especially the ones rooted in how things look rather than what they represent. Choosing vision over vanity, we begin to prioritize substance over style in every area of life.

This shift brings to mind a powerful biblical account of how God confronted pride in the heart of King Nebuchadnezzar. Standing atop his palace, the king looked out over the grandeur of Babylon and declared, "Is not this great Babylon that I have built...by the might of my power, and for the honour of my majesty?" (Daniel 4:30 KJV) It was a moment steeped in self-glorification.

But heaven had a humbling in store.

God stripped away the illusion of control. The mighty monarch who once wore robes of splendor was reduced to crawling in the fields like an animal—grazing like oxen, soaked with dew, his nails like claws, and his hair matted like feathers. Pride had raised him high, but God's correction brought him low. It remains one of the most sobering portraits of divine humbling in all of Scripture.

Restoration came when his understanding returned. Out of the grass and dew came a new kind of testimony—one shaped not by royal decree but by repentance. Listen to King Nebuchadnezzar's words after his encounter with divine discipline:

"I blessed the most High, and praised and honored him that liveth forever, whose dominion is an everlasting dominion, and his kingdom is from generation to generation. And all the inhabitants of the earth are reputed as nothing: and he doeth according to his will…and none can stay his hand, or say unto him, What doest thou?" (Daniel 4:34–35 KJV)

The king who once gloried in his own majesty now exalted the dominion of God.

Then came his final declaration, a sobering truth I've come to know well:

"Now I Nebuchadnezzar praise and extol and honor the King of heaven…and those that walk in pride he is able to abase" (Daniel 4:37 KJV).

Let his words be more than history—let them be a warning. The same God who humbled a Babylonian king still knows how to deal with pride. Better to humble ourselves under His mighty hand than to be brought low in the fields of affliction.

Let this serve as our caution and our call. The same God who humbled Babylon's proud king still humbles hearts today. We can choose the path of surrender—or be driven to it. It's far better to bow willingly under His mighty hand than to be broken in the grass fields of affliction. The fields are not God's goal—they are His mercy. But humility? That's His invitation.

Discussion Questions for Chapter 5: The Competitive Prison of Pride

Let's Start Here:

Ever catch yourself turning something ridiculous into a competition? Pride has a sneaky way of making *everything* feel like a scoreboard.

What's a moment when you realized you were way more competitive than the situation called for?

Maybe it was:

- Getting *way* too intense during family game night
- Competing to have the worst day or busiest schedule
- Racing someone for the best parking spot (and pretending it didn't matter)
- Feeling a little too invested in who got more likes online

- Trying to one-up someone's vacation, restaurant, or life story
- Secretly wanting to "win" at being the most humble

We're all guilty of those "Why did I care so much about that?!" moments. Let's laugh, reflect, and remember that comparison is a trap—and humility sets us free.

1. The Stranger's Warning

When Pastor Josh was nine, a stranger told him, "Son, you must learn humility." At the time, he didn't understand the weight of those words. Years later, they made sense.

- Can you think of a time someone gave you advice you didn't want to hear—but it turned out to be exactly what you needed?
- How do you recognize the difference between working hard for something and simply receiving it as a gift from God?

2. When Everything Feels Like a Competition

The author describes a season where he viewed life like a scoreboard—someone else's win felt like his loss. That mindset distorted his ability to celebrate others.

- What's the difference between healthy competition and the kind that poisons relationships?
- How can you genuinely rejoice with others even when you're struggling yourself?

3. Pride in Two Forms

Pride isn't always loud and boastful. Sometimes it shows up as insecurity, needing constant validation or comparing yourself to others.

- Do you see pride surface more through overconfidence or through self-doubt?
- How can you become more self-aware without becoming self-absorbed?

Defensiveness at Home

The author's wife once told him, "I can't tell you anything negative about yourself." That moment opened his eyes to how pride had shaped his relationships.

- How do you tend to respond when loved ones give you honest feedback?
- What would it look like to pause, listen, and respond with humility instead of defensiveness?

4. Dealing with the Root, Not Just the Fruit

Instead of just trying to act less competitive or stop comparing himself, the author had to dig deeper and confront pride at the root.

- What "symptoms" of pride show up most often in your life— like needing to be right, struggling to admit fault, or comparing yourself constantly?
- What would it mean to let God deal with the root cause instead of managing the behavior?

Further Reflection:

King Nebuchadnezzar went from boasting on his palace rooftop to crawling in the grass—until humility finally took root in his heart.

- What would it look like for you to choose humility now, before life forces it on you?

CHAPTER 6:
FAMILIAR FACES

*"Be especially careful when you are trying to be good so that
you don't make a performance out of it. It might be good
theater, but the God who made you won't be applauding."*

Matthew 6:1 MSG

Pride is a mask; it covers an injury, but it does not help to heal it.

My twenty-third year of life is a fault line—the before and after of true surrender. Up to that point, my gift had remained dormant, my calling unanswered, and my lifestyle misaligned with the purpose stirring within. But standing at a spiritual crossroads, I made the decision: I was going all in for Jesus, no reservations.

God's first lesson wasn't about ministry or theology, though. It was about worship.

When I was invited to serve at a youth retreat called *Discipleship Now*, I had no idea it would become the catalyst for everything that followed. That weekend, I encountered an atmosphere of worship so authentic, it shattered my religious pretenses. Something woke up in me, and I knew I could no longer settle for Sunday performances or occasional spiritual moments.

In the weeks that followed, I shut myself away with a guitar I barely knew how to play and sang with a voice that would never be invited onstage. Like David, I discovered the essence of worship in those raw, unpolished offerings—just me and God. No audience. No technique. No need to impress. It wasn't about music. It was about posture.

Like David dancing before the ark with an undignified joy, I began to learn that true worship is when we bow—our bodies, our hearts, and our lives—before God. In that hidden place, I discovered something profound: Humility and worship aren't distant cousins; they're identical twins. Authentic worship requires humility, and a humble life is itself an act of worship.

Each time I bowed in that secret place, layers of false identity began to peel away—the performer seeking approval, the gifted one expecting recognition, the called one demanding a platform. Only in that prostrate position could I see clearly: Pride had been wearing countless masks, each one disguising who God created me to be.

The irony wasn't lost on me—*leastness* meant I had to look down to see up, become small to grow, and surrender control to find direction. In worship's humble posture, I didn't lose my identity; I finally discovered it.

In those early days of surrender, I felt weightless—freshly forgiven, deeply stirred, and joyfully unburdened. It was as if I had stepped into a new life with no baggage. And in many ways, I had. But what I didn't realize then was that some wounds don't show themselves until the pressure increases.

At first, there was no need to prove myself, no stage to steward, no title to protect. I mistook that peace for full healing. But God, in His wisdom, doesn't leave foundations untested. To make us fit for lasting ministry, He applies pressure—not to crush us, but to expose what's still cracked beneath the surface.

The deeper He called me, the more weight I carried—and the more those hidden fractures began to show. That's when pride emerged—not in arrogance, but in subtle self-reliance, masked beneath achievement and religious performance.

While shepherding souls—whether a few or many—I found myself navigating a dangerous path where achievement became pride's perfect disguise. Validation subtly shifted. It wasn't God's voice I was listening for anymore—it was the applause of results: growing attendance, increasing reach, visible fruit. These metrics became my measuring stick, quietly replacing the pure standard of God's approval.

But the Lord, in His mercy, began exposing the deception. The symptom? A heart quick to take offense. My reactions to criticism—whether explosive outbursts or quiet resentment—revealed pride festering beneath a well-maintained appearance of spiritual maturity. Pride shaped me into someone hypersensitive to correction, quick to retaliate, and resistant to the very reconciliation I preached from the pulpit.

Success can be a smokescreen, blinding us to our condition. It whispers justification:

- "Look at what we've built."
- "See what we've accomplished."
- "Consider our track record."
- "Notice the results."

But these achievements don't correct our course—they often enable unhealthy paths to continue. Success became my substitute for God's approval.

If you find yourself frequently offended, pride likely lurks beneath the surface. But here's the trap: Pride won't let you admit

Pride's favorite calling card is offense.

you're offended. That would mean admitting someone had power to hurt you. So instead, it surfaces as explosive anger, cold resentment, harsh critique, mocking humor, or belittling behavior. These reactions act as armor—protecting a wounded ego while blocking the vulnerability that leads to healing and authentic connection.

Pride makes us hypersensitive to comments, quick to take offense, slow to forgive, ready to retaliate, and resistant to reconciliation. This defensive posture turns constructive feedback into perceived attacks, making genuine growth nearly impossible and allowing relationships to deteriorate under the weight of unresolved tensions.

Accomplishment after accomplishment left my spirit empty. Each victory only revealed more mountains to conquer. The very successes I had chased became thorns in my soul—proof that something was off in my walk with God, even if I couldn't name it yet. I was blind to the imbalance, until the Holy Ghost began to deal with my heart.

A life built on the desire for human approval—or the fear of shame—is ultimately anchored in the sinking sand of pride. The Lord showed me I had to relinquish my need for control and embrace humility in every setting. He began teaching me to seek His wisdom, not

> **True growth doesn't come from being esteemed by people. It comes from bowing before Jesus.**

recognition. Not applause. Not affirmation from others the room.

When we build our identity on roles or achievements, we risk being controlled by them. And when those positions are removed—when the applause stops—our sense of self can collapse. Whether we're driven by achievement, recognition, or the need to feel indispensable, identity rooted in anything external will always be unstable. Pride pushes us to extremes—either inflated confidence or paralyzing insecurity. Either way, it distorts who we really are.

There is no balance or lasting peace in a pride-fueled identity. This "conditional identity" is where many of us live addicted to titles, roles, and the sense of being needed. But the cure isn't more responsibility; it's deeper surrender. We return to prayer. We root ourselves in the Word. Humility makes space for God to do the work no title ever could. The New Testament reminds us that our calling flows not from our position, but from our identity in Christ:

"This means that anyone who belongs to Christ has become a new person. The old life is gone; a new life has begun!" (2 Corinthians 5:17 NLT)

When we lose sight of that foundational truth, we drift into competition, comparison, and distraction—territorial battles and petty concerns that pull us away from our true purpose.

An authentic life doesn't grow from pride—it emerges from the security of knowing who we are in Christ. That identity is irrefutable, ironclad, undeniable. From the posture of humility, we gain balance, wisdom, and the ability to focus fully on the assignment God has placed before us.

When our identity is rooted in Christ alone, we're no longer burdened with the need to defend, promote, or preserve ourselves. We're free to pour out our lives in service to others—not to prove our worth, but because we know it's already established.

Once we've truly found our identity in Christ, the compulsion to explain, to insert, to prove, begins to fade. The urge to always speak up, to voice every thought, to be heard in every moment—loses its grip. We begin to understand that silence does not make us less. It simply makes space.

Our values and qualifications are no longer shaped by public opinion or crowd affirmation. We are secure in this truth: God enables us to stand. Our identity is not tied to applause, roles, or recognition. It's anchored in the One who called us.

This kind of security gives us permission to do something radical: Be still. Listen. Let others speak. We stop worrying that silence will diminish us, because we know our worth is already established in Christ alone.

It's in quiet spaces that we often hear God most clearly. When we're no longer consumed by the need to assert ourselves, we make room for the Spirit to move—room for revelation, correction, and transformation. Our confidence no longer rests in how persuasive or impressive we sound. It's anchored in the unchanging truth that we are beloved children of God.

Imagine someone approaching you, delivering a flood of words, and walking away without giving you a chance to respond. Would you avoid them? Dismiss them? Yet how often do we treat God this way?

What we call prayer is often a monologue—our thoughts, our plans, our opinions—spoken with little to no space for God to respond, redirect, or speak. Not everything we label as prayer is truly prayer.

When we recite our viewpoints without pausing to listen, present our plans without asking for His direction, and share our opinions without any openness to correction, we miss the essence of true communion. If day after day we emerge from our "prayer time" unchanged, unmoved, and uncorrected, then we haven't really prayed—we've only performed a religious soliloquy. I don't imagine God being impressed by that. Do you?

Scripture reveals that an authentic, humble relationship with God requires just as much listening as speaking. True prayer makes room—for divine interruption, heavenly correction, spiritual direction, and heart transformation. That kind of openness stands in direct contrast to the cynicism that creeps in when pride or disillusionment hardens our hearts.

According to an article on GotQuestions.org, a cynic is someone who believes people are motivated only by self-interest and cannot be trusted. Cynicism carries a deep-rooted contempt for others and a general disbelief in sincerity or goodness. The Bible offers examples of this posture—Jonah, for instance, resented God's mercy toward the Ninevites because he believed they didn't deserve forgiveness.[ix]

The article goes on to explain that cynicism is the opposite of love and hope—both of which are supposed to characterize followers of Christ. A cynical person tends to be fault finding, sarcastic, and pessimistic. These attitudes often spring from pride, emotional injury, or an unchecked inner life.

But Scripture points us to a better way. Christ offers healing for the bitterness that fuels a cynical heart. His grace doesn't just soften us—it redirects us. Instead of standing on the sidelines with critical detachment, we are invited to engage fully: to dare greatly, strive valiantly, and participate in the kind of life that builds others up rather than tearing them down.

"But if you bite and devour one another, beware lest you be consumed by one another!" (Galatians 5:15 NKJV)

When Pride Looks Like Responsibility

One of pride's most deceptive disguises is the compulsion to be everyone's solution. It rarely shows up as arrogance. More often, it masks itself as responsibility, leadership, or care. But underneath that noble exterior is a quiet pressure: the need to fix, solve, and carry what God never asked us to carry.

Pride doesn't always shout. Sometimes it whispers, *"You're the only one who can handle this."* It shows up not when we have a good idea, but when we believe it's the *only* right one. The difference is subtle, but powerful. A good idea invites conversation; the right idea

> True humility brings a liberating truth: We're not anyone's savior—and we were never meant to be.

ix GotQuestions.org. What Is Cynicism? Accessed June 28, 2025 https://www.gotquestions.org/Bible-cynicism.html

shuts it down. A good idea suggests; the right idea demands. One makes room for others; the other centers on self.

When we let go of the need to be the answer, we're freed to share insight without insisting on agreement, to offer help without requiring its use, and to give counsel without controlling the outcome. We can lead without manipulating, guide without gripping, and serve without self-interest.

In this surrendered posture, we trust God's work in others without needing to orchestrate the outcome ourselves. We stop trying to play the role of hero and start honoring the Holy Spirit's process in someone else's life. I didn't always understand this. I had to learn it the hard way—on a quiet Saturday morning over a round of golf.

As the popular saying goes, *"People don't care how much you know until they know how much you care."*

For years, I treated my Saturday golf outings with Richard like personal coaching sessions. I'd played competitive golf in college, so naturally, I felt qualified to "fix" his swing. Every round became a free clinic—commentary on his grip, stance, follow-through. I thought I was helping. But his game never improved, and our friendship started to feel…tight.

One morning, as we teed off, a question hit me: *"How can I add value to this man?"* Not how can I correct him. Not how can I prove I'm right. Just…*how can I serve?*

That day, I shut down the instructor in me. I asked about his family. His business. His life. I stopped correcting and started listening. And something shifted. Richard's shoulders loosened. His swing found rhythm. By the eighteenth hole, he smiled and said something that pierced me: *"I really enjoyed today."*

Four words. That's all it took to reveal how wrong I'd been.

As leadership expert John Maxwell has noted, *"Success is when you add value to yourself. Significance is when you add value to others."* I had confused being helpful with being right. But when I laid down my need to be the expert and just became a present friend, our friendship—and his swing—both improved.

That moment taught me something deeper than golf. Humility isn't about disappearing—it's about asking, *"How can I guide without needing to be the hero?"* Like the friend of the bridegroom in John 3:29, our role is to point people to Jesus and then step aside.

For too long, I thought I was the main character in Richard's journey. But when I stepped out of the spotlight, God did what I never could. His transformation wasn't about my skill—it was about my surrender.

When we release our grip, we create space for God to be God. His ways are higher than ours. His timing may surprise us. His solution may come from someone else entirely. And sometimes, His plan won't include our involvement at all. His exclusion of us in the moment isn't rejection. It's refinement. A reminder that the outcome never depended on us in the first place. He expects us to trust Him to fix it.

Letting go opens the door for divine wisdom to unfold in ways we never anticipated. It gives others room to struggle, grow, and develop maturity. When we step in too quickly, we may rob them of the very lessons that would make them spiritually resilient.

Stepping back isn't stepping away. It's stepping *aside* so that the spotlight can shine where it belongs. When we stop filling every space with our voice, we begin to hear the thoughts, wisdom, and insight God has distributed among His people. Humility doesn't require silence, but it does require space—space for God to move, and for others to grow.

Face of Insecurity

Insecurity is pride in disguise. It's a spiritual deception that says, *"You're not enough,"* while simultaneously craving constant validation. It wears the mask of inadequacy, but the engine beneath it is still pride—just dressed in different clothes.

I used to think my insecurity was a kind of humility—proof that I was aware of my flaws and careful not to think too highly of myself. But as the years passed and my responsibilities grew, I noticed something troubling: No matter how much affirmation I received, it was never enough. No achievement could quiet the voice that said, *"You're still not good enough."*

And then came the revelation:

> ### Insecurity isn't the opposite of pride—it's just pride with a wounded voice.

Arrogance says, *"I'm the best."* Insecurity says, *"I'm the worst."* But both keep the focus on *self*. Pride is self-exaltation; insecurity is self-obsession. Either way, we remain at the center of our own universe.

This became clearest in how I responded to correction. I presented myself as teachable, but inside I was devastated by the slightest critique. That wasn't humility—it was pride wounded by exposure. A truly humble heart receives correction as an opportunity to grow. Mine took it as an attack.

Even my hunger for affirmation was a symptom. I pursued praise like a starving man searching for food. Compliments brought temporary relief, but never lasting peace. That constant craving wasn't a sign of humility—it was pride's unquenchable thirst.

Healing began when I understood this truth: Humility isn't thinking less of yourself—it's thinking of yourself less. True humility is not insecure. It's grounded, outward-facing, and anchored in God's view, not man's opinion.

Freedom came not when I finally *felt* worthy, but when I stopped trying to *prove* worthiness. In surrender, I found what I had been chasing all along—not the fleeting approval that insecurity demands, but the deep peace humility offers.

When Insecurity Speaks Loudest

At the heart of rude, abrasive behavior often lies a deep-seated insecurity. When someone feels the need to assert themselves aggressively or dismissively, it usually points to an internal lack of confidence or completeness.

Scripture tells us in Colossians that we are "complete in Him"—fully secure in our identity and standing before God. But when we don't rest in that truth, we begin to compensate. We try to assert control, dominate conversations, or shut others down—not because we're strong, but because we're afraid to be exposed.

Rudeness becomes a mask for the perceived weakness we don't want anyone to see. Whether its root is arrogance or inferiority, the driving force is the same: the need to prove we matter. Pride whispers, *"I have to assert myself over you, because I don't feel confident in who I am."* This defensive posture only deepens the insecurity it's trying to hide. But there's a better way.

True strength is a quiet confidence that flows from knowing we are complete in Christ. When that settles in us, we don't have to match rudeness with rudeness. We can respond with grace, patience, and unexpected gentleness. We're no longer reactive, because our worth isn't tied to how others treat us.

This kind of inner security allows us to extend empathy where others extend hostility. It makes space for compassion even in confrontation. And in that space, hearts can begin to soften, and walls can begin to fall.

The antidote to rudeness is not returning fire—it's modeling the calm, grounded confidence that comes from knowing who you are in Christ. That's the posture that defuses tension and speaks life into those who are still wrestling with their own insecurities.

Insecurity rarely stays quiet. Left unchecked, it turns outward—fueling our need to measure ourselves against others. What begins as private self-doubt quickly becomes public striving. We compare our calling, our influence, our success, even our struggles, trying to figure out where we rank. Scripture makes it plain: "They that measure themselves by themselves, and compare themselves among themselves, are not wise" (2 Corinthians 10:12 KJV).

Comparison clouds our vision. It makes us forget who we are and blinds us to the grace we've been given. And what we don't see clearly, we can't steward well.

As the anonymous saying reminds us, *"Comparison is the thief of joy."* One of the saddest outcomes of constant measuring is how it shrinks our sense of worth. It robs us silently, convincing us that what we have is never enough and that who we are is always just a little less than someone else.

This downward spiral leads us to hide our vulnerabilities, envy others' success, and doubt God's provision. Pride becomes our counterfeit jewelry—something shiny we wear to prove our value, even though it holds no real worth. Like costume gems, it may glitter in certain light, but it cannot withstand pressure or scrutiny.

It's no accident that God ends the Ten Commandments not with murder or adultery, but with coveting:

"You shall not covet…" (Exodus 20:17).

This final command speaks directly to the heart. Comparison is the seedbed of covetousness, and from it grows resentment, discontentment, and pride. What the Old Testament called *covetousness*, we've rebranded as *ambition* or *aspiration*, but the root remains: dissatisfaction with what God has given.

Comparison tells us we're missing out, that others are ahead, and that our lives are somehow insufficient. It dresses itself in socially acceptable language, but it still poisons the soul.

Pride and comparison feed each other. When we feel smaller through comparison, pride rushes in to compensate—offering inflated confidence, defensiveness, or a critical spirit. But pride is demanding. It requires constant upkeep. We keep reassessing our standing, outpacing others, trying to prove something that it was never ours to earn.

The cycle breaks only when we face the truth: Our worth was never found in our relative position to others—it was secured from the very beginning by the unchanging love of the One who created us.

The Freedom Path

True worth is not found in measuring up—it's found in looking up. It's not achieved by comparing ourselves to others, but by resting in God's specific design for our lives.

The antidote to covetousness isn't getting more—it's wanting less and thanking more.

Pride wears countless masks. It chains us with false identities, each one designed to keep us focused on self—whether through inflated ego or self-diminishing doubt. Either way, pride traps us in a shallow orbit around our own reflection. But humility breaks the cycle.

Our journey toward humility doesn't begin with fixing our image—it begins with surrendering it. Only when we step outside the exhausting swirl of self-assessment can we find the peace Christ promised. Joy isn't found in being better than someone else—it's found in being fully alive to the wonder of God's love and the needs of those around us.

Of all pride's disguises, spiritual pride may be the most dangerous. It turns virtue into poison, whispering that struggle equals failure and that real faith means never appearing weak. When under its control we are compelled to hide our flaws, to project confidence, and to mask our battles.

True spirituality invites vulnerability. It says, *"You don't have to be perfect to be present."* The moments we try to appear the strongest are often the ones when we're most isolated. Our humanity doesn't disqualify us from holiness—it's the very ground where grace takes root. Salvation is not about image. It's about transformation.

When we admit we're not okay, we're not confessing weakness—we're making space for God to show up. As Jesus said of Lazarus, "This sickness will not end in death. No, it is for God's glory so that God's Son may be glorified through it" (John 11:4).

Brokenness is not a liability—it's a canvas.

We spend so much energy curating the version of ourselves we think others want to see. Like social media profiles, we polish the exterior and hide the unfinished places. But God isn't looking for performance. He's looking for surrender.

Some battles weren't given to us so we could win. Some were given so that He could be glorified through our weakness.

Humility acknowledges both truths at once: *"I need help"* and *"I'm still loved."* It stops the swinging between perfectionism and resignation. It brings balance—neither anxiously striving nor silently retreating. That's the freedom that comes from resting in Christ.

The wilderness becomes our classroom. Like Jesus in the desert, we learn to lean on the Word, not willpower. Scripture doesn't just inform—it transforms. It tells us who God is, who we are, and what has already been secured through Christ.

Constant renewal of the mind dismantles doubt and reminds us that our identity is not based on performance, but on position. Worship becomes a radical act—not of defeat, but of alignment. We bow not because we've lost, but because we understand.

> Humility gives us the courage to admit need and the confidence to rest in Christ's sufficiency.

Humility gives us the courage to admit need and the confidence to rest in Christ's sufficiency. That kind of surrender is not weakness—it's a breakthrough.

A revelation struck me one day as I knelt before God: Worship is not performance—it's posture. To bow is to acknowledge that there is Someone greater. To give up is to relinquish control. To yield is to trust beyond your understanding.

And in that sacred yielding, strength is born.

Each time you bow, you open a door to rise. Every surrender becomes a seed of transformation. What looks like the death of your old self is not a loss—it's a rebirth. Brought low, yet lifted. Emptied, yet filled. Flat on your face, yet more alive than ever.

The bottom line is that we don't lose ourselves in humility. Instead we finally find who we were created to be. Pride may wear many faces, but every one of them hides us from the freedom we were made for. Only when we lay them down in humility do we finally see the face of Christ—and, in Him, our truest selves.

Discussion Questions for Chapter 6: Familiar Faces

Let's Start Here:

Pride doesn't always show up loud and obvious—it's a master of disguise. Sometimes it hides behind helpfulness, humility, or high standards.

Can you think of a moment when your pride showed up wearing a "harmless" mask?

Maybe it looked like:

- Offering advice to be "helpful" (but really wanting to sound smart)

- Feeling just a *little* smug about your taste in TV, food, or music

- Being low-key irritated when someone ignored your clearly better way

- Casually mentioning how humble you are (more than once)

We're all guilty of those "Oh…that was pride, wasn't it?" moments. Let's call them out, laugh a little, and keep growing in grace.

1. Pride's Many Disguises

The chapter reveals how pride wears different masks—like cynicism, the need to rescue everyone, rudeness, comparison, insecurity, or even appearing overly spiritual.

- Which of these disguises do you recognize in yourself?
- How does naming these patterns help you address the real issue rather than just the symptoms?

2. When Success Becomes Your Report Card

The author admits that ministry growth became a way to validate his worth, instead of simply receiving it as God's blessing.

- How can you tell when you're enjoying the good things in life versus using them to prove your value?
- What would it look like to measure your worth by God's view instead of what seems impressive?

3. The "I Can Fix Everything" Mindset

The chapter challenges the belief that our ideas are not just good—but the only right ones—and exposes our desire to be everyone's hero.

- When have you experienced the freedom of stepping back and letting go of control?
- How can you offer help to others without taking ownership of their outcomes?

4. Insecurity: Pride in Disguise

One powerful insight in this chapter is that insecurity isn't humility—it's pride turned inward. Both keep self at the center.

- Does this shift how you view your own insecurity?
- What's the difference between honest self-awareness and being consumed with how you compare to others?

5. Are You Praying—Or Just Talking?

The author asks us to reflect on whether we're truly praying or just performing a monologue before God.

- How could you make more space for God to actually respond when you pray?

- What might change if you listened in prayer as much as you spoke?

Further Reflection

Humanity as a Pathway to Holiness

The chapter reminds us that humanity is not a barrier to holiness; it is the pathway. You don't have to pretend to be perfect to grow spiritually.

- How does that truth challenge the pressure to appear like you have it all together?

- What would it look like to be genuinely honest about your struggles—in your friendships, in your faith, and in your church community?

CHAPTER 7:
SACRED DESCENT

"Therefore humble yourselves under the mighty hand of God, that He may exalt you in due time."

1 Peter 5:6 NKJV

In quiet moments of reflection, when the world's noise fades to a whisper, I've come to understand that true greatness is not found in what we claim to be, but in what we're willing to admit we are not. Humility, I've learned, is not weakness cloaked in virtue—it's wisdom in its most honest form.

My journey has been shaped as much by stumbles as by successes, and most of my lessons came not through applause but through the sting of failure. From ordinary beginnings to unexpected turns, I've discovered that real strength rises when we embrace our limitations. Our most meaningful connections often form in the places where we lay our masks down. This is not a story of conquest, but of surrender—not about rising above others, but finding a steady foundation within myself. The most powerful transformation came when I chose to bow to truths greater than my ambition.

> Our most meaningful connections often form in the places where we lay our masks down.

There was a season when I had opportunities to step into prominent ministry roles—pastoral offers in cities like Lafayette, Lake Charles, and New Orleans. On paper, they looked like the breakthrough I had prayed for. But something in my spirit held back. I felt the Lord asking me to stay—under my father's leadership, in a place that didn't offer platform but offered something deeper: refinement. Saying no wasn't easy. It felt like I was turning down open doors. But I've learned that not every open door is divine. Not every elevation is right on time. What looked like delay was actually protection. God was purifying my motives in the waiting, preparing me for a different kind of strength—one rooted in surrender, not recognition.

The revelation didn't come with thunder—it arrived as a whisper that shook everything in me. After years of pleading for breakthrough, God spoke a truth that shifted my entire posture: *"When I can purify your motives in the waiting that's when your breakthrough will begin to unfold."*

Those words pierced through my expectations and brought clarity to every delay, every closed door, every stretch of silence. I began to see that the pace of my breakthrough was often tied to how quickly I would let God deal with what was misaligned in me. Instead of asking, *"When, Lord?"* I started asking, *"What?"*

What in me still needs to change?
What must be surrendered?
What has to die?

These pages aren't a celebration of achievements—they're a record of what happened when I finally got out of my own way. They tell the story of a soul unraveling, one layer at a time, until there was nothing left but surrender. And in that surrender, I learned that the waiting wasn't punishment. The waiting *was* the answer. It was in the waiting that I became someone who could receive—open handed—not just the gifts I longed for, but the Giver Himself.

> **It was in the waiting that I became someone who could receive—open handed—not just the gifts I longed for, but the Giver Himself.**

My prayers shifted from desperate cries for breakthrough to quiet invitations for revelation.

"Okay, Lord—let's get to work."

I came to realize the real work wasn't in the waiting room, but in the mirror—where He invited me to examine my motives and yield my heart.

So I began asking harder questions—ones that didn't flatter my image but confronted it.

What parts of my character still needed refinement?
Where was I still driven more by ambition than obedience?

What did I fear losing if I released control?
What did I hope to gain that God had not promised?
And perhaps most importantly: *Why was I still in such a hurry?*

These weren't easy questions to sit with. But they became tools in the hands of a gentle God who was less interested in polishing my image and more committed to forming my heart.

There's a thread of impatience woven into our pride. It pushes us to hurry, to grasp for opportunities, to prove we're ready even when we're not. It thrives on the rush to be seen, to get ahead, to grab the mic before someone else does. But humility moves at a different pace. It doesn't scramble for recognition or sprint toward affirmation. Rooted in something deeper than performance, it's unhurried—and comfortable in obscurity—because it trusts that God is just as present in the shadows as He is on the stage. He buries us not to forget us, but to form us. In His hands, obscurity is never punishment—it's preparation.

Every morning became an opportunity for surrender; each obstacle, a chance for growth. I stopped waiting for the breakthrough and started preparing for it. Breakthrough wasn't a distant event I hoped would arrive. It was something I had to become ready to carry. That readiness always began with a daily giving over of my will, my want, and my way. I started to see that the delays weren't detours. They were divine appointments meant to dig deeper into my heart, revealing what still needed to be laid down.

Along the way, I've discovered that authentic lowliness isn't announced—it's demonstrated. It doesn't come through grand declarations but through small, consistent acts of "leastness." I found deep inspiration in how Jesus set aside divine privilege. He didn't demand attention or proclaim His greatness. Instead, He quietly poured out power through service—through acts that required no spotlight and offered no applause.

When I release my expectations, rights, and privileges for the sake of others and for purposes beyond myself, I hear the echo of John the Baptist: "He must increase, but I must decrease" (John 3:30 KJV). In these moments, I find freedom—not the kind that demands a platform, but the kind that loosens the grip of self-importance. The more I surrender, the more I see that the path to fullness begins with emptying.

In choosing to become less, I begin to live more like Christ—quietly, purposefully, and with a strength that doesn't need to be seen to be real.

While we gravitate to chasing recognition and acquiring status, Jesus showed us something radically different. The Creator of all things walked among the broken, not above them. He set aside glory to serve, to stoop, to wash feet, and to remain silent in the face of injustice. He never grasped for power—He gave it up. That kind of surrender doesn't fit our culture's definition of greatness, but it is the very heartbeat of the gospel.

God's wisdom turns our ladders upside down. As Isaiah reminds us, His thoughts soar far above ours. In His kingdom, greatness is marked not by prominence but by presence. By making a lasting impact through modeling compassion, forgiveness, and the quiet courage to serve when no one sees. What the world dismisses as weakness, God calls strength. What human reasoning mocks as foolish, heaven celebrates as power.

Psalm 18:35 NKJV says, "Your right hand has held me up; Your gentleness has made me great." At first glance, it almost seems like a contradiction. How could gentleness—not strength or discipline—be the

> **In God's kingdom, greatness doesn't climb—it bows.**

thing that makes someone great? But the Hebrew behind that word for *gentleness* reveals something rich in meaning and strong in application. It speaks of a deliberate lowering, like a parent or nursemaid stooping to care for a child. It's not weakness—it's intentional condescension in mercy. God made David great not by exalting him immediately, but by stooping low to meet him in his need. His greatness didn't begin with a throne—it began with the kindness of a God who lowers Himself to lift us up. When we reflect that same nature—when we stoop in love, in patience, in compassion—we step into true kingdom greatness.

Jesus didn't wield authority through force or control. He didn't manipulate outcomes or assert dominance to prove His position. Instead, He knelt. He served. He listened. He walked with people others overlooked. The authority He carried wasn't loud—but it was undeniable. It came from a life aligned with the Father, from a heart secure enough to lay itself down. His power wasn't diminished by gentleness—it was revealed through it. That's the kind of authority heaven recognizes. And it's the kind God still honors today.

Humility doesn't just shape how we lead—it shapes how we apologize, how we listen, and how we respond when we're misunderstood. It's what allows us to receive correction without defensiveness and to acknowledge impact even when our intentions were good. I used to think strength meant always having the right answer. Now I know it means having the right posture. Humility doesn't eliminate confidence—it purifies it. It anchors our identity in Christ, not in being right or being praised.

When the Spirit of God cultivates humility in us, it changes everything. We stop needing to be the smartest person in the room. We stop measuring ourselves by who's ahead or behind. We begin to value obedience over applause, and transformation over titles. Humility invites us to live open handed and open hearted, trusting that God knows how to raise us in the right time—and how to prune us when it's not.

When I look at the life of Joseph, I see a man God trusted with influence—but only after He had trained him in obscurity. Before Joseph ever interpreted Pharaoh's dream, he had to endure betrayal, slavery, and prison. His gifts were evident early on, but his character was forged in the silence between promise and fulfillment. God wasn't just preparing a position for Joseph—He was preparing Joseph for the position. And when the moment came, Joseph didn't seek revenge or recognition. He wept. He forgave. He used his authority to preserve life. That's the kind of strength humility produces.

Joseph didn't need to announce his greatness—his life revealed it. He wasn't trying to prove a point; he was living out a purpose. His story reminds me that when God truly exalts someone, they don't have to strive to stay there. They know who placed them, and they know why. Joseph carried power without being controlled by it. He remembered the pit, the prison, the pain—and it shaped how he held the palace. That's what sacred descent does: prepares us to carry influence without losing integrity.

> Surrender isn't about losing your voice. It's about learning to steward it.

Surrender isn't about losing your voice. It's about learning to steward it. It doesn't demand silence, but it does demand releasing ownership. This kind of posture doesn't weaken boldness; it purifies it. It gives words weight because they come from a place of alignment, not ego. It's knowing when to speak, how to speak, and why it matters. A voice yielded to God becomes an instrument of healing not a weapon for self-promotion.

This is the sacred descent—downward, deeper, hidden. Not because we're being diminished, but because we're being shaped. God doesn't rush the process. He's not after polished performances; He's after surrendered hearts. The way up in the kingdom is always down, and every step lower is an invitation to become more like Christ. We don't disappear in the descent. We become anchored in what matters most.

Discussion Questions for Chapter 7: Sacred Descent

Let's Start Here:

Waiting can feel frustrating—but sometimes, it's where the real magic happens.

Can you think of a time when being stuck in a *waiting season* (literally or figuratively) ended up bringing something surprisingly good?

Maybe it was:

- Sitting in traffic but having the best heart-to-heart
- Waiting in line and striking up a meaningful conversation
- A flight delay that turned into an unexpected adventure
- Waiting on results and finding space to pray, reflect, or reset
- A slow season at work that opened the door to a hobby or friendship
- Being stuck at home that led to unexpected rest or connection

We're looking for those *"waiting room wins"*—moments when delay turned into a blessing in disguise.

1. When Waiting Becomes the Answer

The author writes that God told him: *"When I can purify your motives in the waiting that's when your breakthrough will begin."*

- What are you waiting for right now?

- Instead of asking, "When will this happen?" how might things change if you asked, "What do You want to shape in me while I wait?"

2. Putting on Humility Daily

Peter urges believers to "clothe yourselves with humility"—like putting on work clothes that stay on all day.

- What would it look like to intentionally choose humility each morning?

- What parts of your day—or your personality—push back against that choice?

3. Joseph's Stripped-Down Journey

Before Joseph stepped into his purpose, he lost the robe from his father and the clothes of his captivity. God stripped away the external labels to reveal a deeper identity.

- What things do you use to define yourself—career, talent, reputation, relationships—that God might be asking you to hold more loosely?

- How can you tell the difference between healthy confidence and needing other people's approval?

4. Speaking with Purpose or Ego?

Before David faced Goliath, his words weren't about his own greatness—they reflected trust in God and a desire to serve.

- In your conversations, are you more focused on helping others or being impressive?
- Can you remember a time you had to choose between showing off and truly serving?

5. Your Pit Season

Joseph's lowest seasons weren't wasted—they were preparation. The pit, the prison, the forgotten years, all of it shaped him for the palace.

- Think back: How has a hard season in your life actually prepared you for something greater?
- If you're in a difficult place now, how might God be using it to get you ready for what's next?

Further Reflection

Thinking of Yourself Less

"Humility isn't thinking less of yourself—it's thinking of yourself less."

- How does this reshape your understanding of humility?
- What's the difference between being aware of your strengths and weaknesses—and being consumed by how you're perceived?

CHAPTER 8:
THE UPSIDE-DOWN KINGDOM

"For whoever exalts himself will be humbled, and he who humbles himself will be exalted."

Luke 14:11 NKJV

"You can ask God to make you humble, and he can make you humble without humiliating you."—Reverend Joel Urshan

I was brittle enough that facing a fault, receiving a hard truth, undid me, just split me like a rotted seam on an old shirt. Now, I view confronting the ugly in me as a reshaping of God's design, remodel of the fragile façade I'd constructed. What once felt like personal attacks—statements that shocked, hurt, or caught me off guard—have become unexpected gifts of growth. It may sting at first, but like the prick of the needle is momentary, the medicine it delivers brings a healing I can never produce on my own. Each confrontation with truth is an invitation to see myself clearly, beyond the stories I've told or the image I've polished. As false layers fall away, roots of humility can now intertwine in the soil of my humanity, choking out the vines of self-deception—until nothing deceitful remains hidden.

This ability to receive hard truths didn't grow out of a workbook or leadership podcast. It was born in the quiet places where I spent time with God.

Ephesians 3:16 NKJV says, "...that He would grant you, according to the riches of His glory, to be strengthened with might through His Spirit in the inner man."

That strength changed the terrain of my soul. Slowly, the need to earn approval lost its grip on me. I stopped living for other people's praise—and started living free. Perfectionism lost its power. People-pleasing no longer paralyzed me.

Criticism, once a trigger for fear and defensiveness, now meets a quieter spirit—one that's willing to consider what might be true. I'm still learning, but my identity is anchored beyond human judgment. And from that anchor, I've discovered a different kind of strength: one soft enough to stay open, but firm enough not to break when truth arrives.

Here's an unexpected result: The less we need approval, the more freely we give it. And when we give it freely, it often flows back in abundance. This is God's relational design in motion:

- The more we humble ourselves, the more others lift us
- The more we affirm others, the more affirmation finds us
- The more we love without fear, the more love returns
- The more we decrease, the more God increases us

This isn't a strategy—it's a cycle of grace. Not striving, but overflow. Not manipulation, but mutual strengthening.

Understanding humility is a lot like trying to describe someone you love. I could tell you about my wife—her beauty, her spirit, her presence—but if you've never met her, you couldn't pick her out of a crowd. Humility is the same way. It's real, even radiant, but unless you've encountered it, you might not recognize it when you see it.

> When approval is no longer a craving, it becomes a gift we pass freely between hearts rooted in God's strength.

We often chase humility while mislabeling it. Some mistake it for low self-worth—a slumped posture or a silenced voice. But that's not the humility of Christ. Others treat confidence as arrogance, assuming that boldness and humility can't coexist. That misses the mark too.

Pride and humility shape every part of our spiritual lives—every victory and every valley. Yet, like trying to describe a person to someone who's never met them, these qualities are hard to define and even harder to identify at a glance.

Genuine humility isn't something you can grasp through a definition. It must be encountered, experienced, and embodied in relationship with Jesus.

Before we explore what Scripture reveals about pride and humility, we have to clear away the distortions. True humility isn't thinking you're less than everyone else—it's thinking about yourself less, while standing confident in who God created you to be.

If we misunderstand what humility looks like, pride will gladly wear the costume. It will dress itself in self-deprecation, in false modesty, even in religious asceticism, convincing us that our lowered posture is holy, when it's really just another performance.

We don't come to recognize true humility by looking inward. We recognize it by looking to Christ. He is the standard, the pattern, and the perfect picture. Without His example, we will call pride humility and miss the very thing we're meant to embody.

The Journey to Bondage

The story begins in a season of abundance. Through Joseph's favor, God's people found safety in Egypt's fertile land of Goshen. What started as a blessing became home—but over time, that comfort gave way to captivity. As generations passed and favor faded, the land that once sheltered them slowly turned into a place of bondage.

Egypt didn't become a prison overnight, and neither do the strongholds in our lives. Like Israel, we often settle into comfort, unaware that it's shaping us more than we realize. The shift is slow—so slow we don't notice when the blessing begins to bind us. That's the danger of subtle bondage. Not all chains are made of iron.

Some slip around us disguised as convenience, coping, or even personal freedom. A defensive attitude that quietly poisons every relationship. A simmering anger that begins to dictate our tone and reactions. A habit of numbing ourselves through screens that consumes the hours we meant to steward. Or subtle indulgences that, over time, reshape our appetites until they master us. Even patterns we once called harmless—routines, escapes, comforts—can harden into spiritual strongholds.

The things we once turned to for relief begin to rule us. What begins as comfort can end in captivity—quietly, gradually, and then all at once.

The Nondescript Applicator

God's plan to deliver Israel reached its turning point at Passover. After nine plagues failed to move Pharaoh, the final judgment came—but with it, a clear instruction. Every household was to take the blood of a lamb and apply it to their doorposts. But the method of application was more than practical. God required it be done with a common bush.

Why hyssop? It wasn't elegant. It wasn't strong. It was a low, scraggly shrub—ordinary, overlooked, growing in wall cracks and dry places. But that's what God chose. This detail wasn't just functional—it was prophetic. In requiring hyssop, God embedded a pattern: Grace is applied through humility.

The sacrifice had already secured their freedom, but without the act of obedience— without the lowly tool touching both blood and house—the protection wouldn't have been activated. Grace is always available. But humility is what applies it.

> **The blood had the power to save, but it was humility that brought it to the threshold.**

That same pattern threads through Scripture. God uses the lowly to carry out what is holy. He chooses weak vessels to bear His strength— not in spite of their weakness, but because of it. Again and again, God selects the ordinary to carry out the extraordinary, ensuring that no flesh can boast. His strength flows most fully through those who know they can't manufacture it.

The principle still stands: Freedom doesn't come by knowledge alone. It takes both the blood of Christ and the humility to apply it. We can study grace, sing about it, and even preach it—but until humility bridges the gap between what God offers and what we need, the power remains untouched.

Just as hyssop had to touch both the blood and the doorpost, humility connects God's provision to our condition. Without that simple, lowly applicator, even the most powerful grace remains unreceived.

Living in God's grace means walking in favor that doesn't make sense by human standards. But many struggle to stay there—because grace requires a kind of humility that feels unnatural to the flesh. As Jesus said, we must learn from Him. We must choose lowliness. Choose meekness. And until we know who we are in Him, we'll always feel threatened by who others are around us.

That's why humility can become exhausting. When it's not rooted in identity, it turns into a treadmill—constant effort, no rest, no reward. Trying to *act* humble while believing you're "less than" creates something worse than pride: insecurity dressed in religious language. It drives us to compete, to defend, to resist rather than release.

But when God teaches you who you are—through Scripture and through prayer—everything shifts. Confidence rises, but it's quiet. Strong. Secure. You begin to walk in a humility that isn't performative but peaceful. And that's the mystery: to be bold enough to be meek. Grounded enough to let go of the need to be seen.

The hyssop was common. Overlooked. Plentiful. And maybe that's the point. The things that bring us low—correction, surrender, prayer, repentance—they're rarely dramatic. They're everyday brushes with the sacred. And yet, it's through the steady application of what seems common that grace gets worked deep into us.

What changes a life isn't one emotional moment—it's consistent encounters with the divine that result in a softened heart, an open spirit, and a willingness to bend. It's the outcome of the supernatural power of the blood applied to the most ordinary corners of our lives, until nothing remains untouched.

In Matthew 11:29, Jesus offers an invitation: "Take my yoke upon you, and learn from me, for I am gentle and lowly in heart, and you will find rest for your souls." He doesn't just command us to be humble—He invites us to learn humility directly from Him.

That's what makes this invitation so compelling: It's not forced. Jesus doesn't demand that we become humble; He extends the offer. That's the heart of the challenge, right? The choice is ours. God does not impose, He invites us to embrace. It's a posture of the heart we must choose to take.

What Jesus calls "gentle and lowly" isn't weakness. It's the essence of His strength. It's the bedrock of rest—the kind of soul-rest we're desperate for but can't manufacture.

Why doesn't Jesus just *make* us humble? Because humility that costs nothing means nothing. It must be chosen to be real. It's only in surrendering our pride, again and again, that we begin to take on His nature. It's in that low place, we find the rest, identity, and peace we are meant to possess. The path isn't easy—but the fruit is eternal.

Jesus invites us to take His yoke—not just to observe it, not just to admire it, but to step into it. Only then can we begin to learn from Him. Real transformation starts when we choose to link ourselves to Him in trust and obedience. Relationship is the classroom where spiritual growth takes root.

As we stay connected to Jesus, the Holy Spirit begins to teach us—not just with words, but with conviction, correction, and gentle reminders. As John 14:26 tells us, "The Helper, the Holy Spirit…will teach you all things and bring to your remembrance all that I have said to you."

Yoking was never about carrying the load alone. In fact, when two animals are yoked together, they can carry far more than they could on their own. One horse might pull 6,000 pounds—but two can pull 18,000. That's the kind of supernatural multiplication God offers when we surrender to His lead. We don't drag the burden—we walk with Him in step. And in walking with Him, we learn what the world can't teach: the strength of surrender, the honor of humility, the greatness of going low.

The Spirit reminds us again and again. Not through force, but through presence. A teachable spirit makes room for instruction, and instruction brings growth. This isn't a onetime lesson—it's a life-long process of being reshaped, re-centered, refined.

The question is still ours to answer: Will we submit to His yoke? Will we walk at His pace? Will we stay humble enough to keep learning? Because in that posture—one of surrendered teachability—we access the deep wisdom of the Spirit. As Proverbs 25:15 says, "By long forbearing is a prince persuaded." Patience and humility carry more power than we know. The strength that prevails is the kind that forgets itself and follows God.

Relationships are at the center of our design—woven into the fabric of what it means to be human. From the beginning, God created us for connection: with Him, with others, with ourselves. Subtle and slippery, pride has a way of unraveling what was meant to be whole. It distances. It defends. It divides.

> **Where pride isolates, humility builds bridges.**

On the other hand, a lowly nature mends. It draws close. It opens doors. It allows us to be known without pretense and to know others without judgment. Where pride isolates, humility builds bridges. It becomes the soil where genuine connection grows.

If transformation is what we seek, we won't find it in self-improvement or image management. We'll find it in humility—in the quiet willingness to lower ourselves so God can raise up something lasting.

Let's consider the example of Jesus—how He endured suffering without retreating from His purpose. Hebrews 12:2 KJV reminds us: "Looking unto Jesus, the author and finisher of our faith; who for the joy that was set before him endured the cross, despising the shame..."

Jesus didn't embrace the pain, but He didn't run from it either. He despised the shame—refusing to let it define Him or derail Him. What others heaped on Him didn't change what He knew about Himself or about His mission.

How was that possible? Philippians 2:5–7 ESV holds the answer: "Have this mind among yourselves, which is yours in Christ Jesus...he emptied himself, taking the form of a servant."

Though He was equal with God, Jesus chose the posture of a servant. He laid down privilege, position, and power—and took up humility. That mindset made endurance possible.

Real endurance isn't about gritting your teeth and pushing through. It's about releasing control, laying down ego, and fully trusting the Father's will. That's the path Jesus walked—and it's the one He invites us to follow.

The road isn't smooth, but the outcome is priceless. For the joy set before us, we can walk it—confident that humility isn't weakness, and surrender isn't loss. It's how we endure with grace.

Jesus endured unimaginable hardship with a steady peace—because He had nothing to prove. He wasn't trying to protect a reputation or build a platform. There was no image to maintain, no persona to defend. He walked in total freedom because His identity was secure.

The Apostle Paul echoed this mindset when he wrote in Philippians 3:14, "I press toward the mark for the prize of the high calling of God in Christ Jesus." But Paul knew that pressing forward came with a cost. Just verses earlier, he spoke of "fellowship with [Christ's] sufferings." The path to purpose runs through surrender.

Only when we let God mark our lives—when we release control over how we're seen, measured, or remembered—can the Holy Spirit begin the deep work of transformation. That kind of freedom doesn't come from striving. It comes from leastness.

The strongest people in the room aren't trying to be impressive—they're too secure to need the spotlight. And in that hidden strength, they make the greatest impact.

When we pour ourselves out in service, something unexpected happens: We get filled. That's the mystery of a humble heart—it gives freely, and in the giving, it grows.

> **When we pour ourselves out in service, something unexpected happens: We get filled.**

Selfless giving only happens when we're secure. If we're still trying to prove our worth, we'll turn every relationship into a fulcrum—leveraging others to lift ourselves. Until we're anchored in who we are in Christ, we'll relate to others as if they're obstacles or stepping stones. As long as we're operating from shady transactional friendships, we won't lift anyone else for the sole purpose of seeing them shine.

When our identity is anchored, everything shifts. We become steady enough to turn outward—to become the shoulders others can stand on. That's what it means to lead like Christ: to make others great, even when no one sees it.

Humility unlocks that power. It turns us from competitors into collaborators. It frees us to celebrate others without feeling smaller ourselves. It's not just good character—it's kingdom strategy.

We begin to see people through the lens of God's love, not through the fog of our own insecurity. And that changes everything. We lead, follow, forgive, and connect from a different posture.

When our hearts are grounded in humility, we stop comparing and start connecting. We let go of the need to impress, and we lean into the call to bless. We don't have to fight for position—we're free to show up with kindness, to serve without needing credit, to forgive without keeping score.

This kind of heart creates space—for joy to take root, for peace to settle in, for others to grow. The fruit of a life yoked with Christ becomes unmistakable: love, joy, peace, patience, kindness, goodness, faithfulness, gentleness, and self-control (Galatians 5). Not manufactured. Not performed. Just the natural overflow of a surrendered life.

And the beautiful part? When humility is real, we don't have to announce it. Our lives will speak loud enough.

Discussion Questions for Chapter 8: The Upside-Down Kingdom

Let's Start Here:

God's kingdom doesn't always follow our logic—sometimes the "worst" moments end up being the best things that could've happened.

Can you think of a time when something that felt like a setback actually turned out to be a setup for something better?

Maybe it was:

- A job or opportunity that didn't work out—but something better did

- A canceled plan that opened a new, unexpected door

- A mistake that turned into a lesson you needed

- A failure that helped you find your real purpose

- A humbling moment that led to healing, connection, or growth

We're looking for those *"plot twist"* moments—when life flipped upside down and you realized God was at work all along.

1. The Hyssop Principle

God used a simple, lowly plant (hyssop) to apply the Passover blood—showing that humility is what helps us actually receive His grace.

- Think about a time when you had to swallow your pride to ask for help or admit you were wrong.

- How did that humility open the door for God to work?

- Where might pride be blocking you from receiving what God wants to give you right now?

2. Receiving Hard Truths as Gifts

The author learned to see tough feedback as a gift, not an attack on his ego.

- Think of a time recently when someone told you something that was hard to hear.

- Did you get defensive—or were you able to listen?

- What would help you pause and consider their words instead of rushing to defend yourself?

3. God's Upside-Down Way

The chapter says when we stop needing people's approval, we're free to encourage others—and ironically, we often receive more love in return.

- Where are you still trying to prove yourself or earn validation?

- How might your relationships change if you felt fully secure in who God says you are?

4. Going It Alone vs. Team Jesus

Jesus says, "Take My yoke." Like two horses pulling together, we can do more with Him than alone.

- What areas of your life are you trying to handle on your own instead of inviting Jesus in?

- What's the difference between trying to be humble on your own and learning humility from Jesus?

5. Your Scars Tell a Story

The author says our wounds and failures aren't shameful—they're proof of how God rescues and heals.

- What past hurts or mistakes still make you feel ashamed?
- How might God want to use that part of your story to help someone else?
- What would it look like to own your scars as testimony instead of hiding them?

Further Reflection

The chapter invites us to resist the pull of pride and platform in favor of hidden obedience.

- Have you ever felt God asking you to stay in a place that didn't boost your ego—but grew your character?
- Have you ever had to choose between something that felt good for your reputation and something God was calling you to instead?
- What did that experience teach you about following God versus chasing what looks impressive?

CHAPTER 9:

REMARKABLE

"And He said to me, 'My grace is sufficient for you, for My strength is made perfect in weakness.' Therefore most gladly I will rather boast in my infirmities, that the power of Christ may rest upon me."

2 Corinthians 12:9 NKJV

"Ouch! That's going to leave a mark."

Romans 6:9 NKJV unveils a profound revelation: "Knowing that Christ, having been raised from the dead, dies no more." Christ's resurrection wasn't merely a conquest over death—it was a declaration of complete dominion. And that triumph isn't just part of His story; it becomes the divine blueprint for our transformation.

When God pulls us out of addiction's grip, the devastation of divorce, the chains of lust, or the lonely prison of pride, it's not just about escape. We are being marked—etched by the same resurrection power that overcame death itself.

Once sources of pain, these marks become—through God's redemption—the very features that make us remarkable. He doesn't erase our wounds; He transforms them into evidence of His craftsmanship. Each scar testifies to a bondage that once felt permanent but now points to our spiritual inheritance—freedom secured through Christ's decisive victory.

We don't just survive—we emerge with spiritual authority over what once held us captive. The very experiences that threatened to define us through devastation become, in His hands, the defining elements of our testimony.

This is the mystery of divine marking: The wounds that once cut deepest become, through surrender, what sets us apart. We are not remarkable in spite of our scars, but because of how God has repurposed them for His glory.

Transformed by Divine Marking

God doesn't define us by our achievements or accolades. He marks us by the character formed in the hidden places—where endurance was forged, where pride was broken, where faith held in the dark. These are the places that catch His attention. When the world scans for talent and success, He looks for surrender. And in His mercy, He places His mark not on our résumé but on our resilience. No applause required.

These divine markings reshape us, not through our striving but through our submission. The scars and experiences that once seemed to diminish us become, in His hands, the very features that make us remarkable—not remarkable in the world's spotlight, but a remarking that comes by a kind of spiritual grit only grace builds.

How can we determine if our identity is growing toward Christ? The evidence is clear through unmistakable markers:

- Others are lifted higher while we decrease;
- God's name receives the glory that once fed our ego;
- Lives around us find healing through our brokenness;
- Our deepest joy springs from the success of others rather than from our own recognition;
- And perhaps most tellingly, the spotlight that once seemed essential now holds no appeal.

These are the signs of a soul reshaped by grace—where identity is no longer anchored in applause, but in surrender. The more God marks us, the less we clamor to be seen. The quieter our posture becomes, the clearer His voice sounds. The need to be noticed dissolves in the presence of divine purpose.

God often selects leaders from among the hidden—not because they pursued leadership, but because they have shown they can handle it without being corrupted by it. Their identity remains anchored in the One who elevated them, not in the elevation itself. This is the mystery of remarkable living: Those who become genuinely significant have ceased striving for significance altogether.

We can work without recognition, celebrate when others receive praise for our efforts, find joy in team success over personal acclaim, and serve without needing acknowledgment. This is the hidden path of the humble—finding fulfillment not in the spotlight but in the shadow of the cross.

> Spiritual and emotional maturity shows up when we no longer need credit to feel valued.

God's marking process often begins where our ambition ends.

When we release our need to be seen, He takes up the pen and begins writing something better. The wounds, setbacks, and disappointments we might have wanted to forget become, in His hands, the very markings that make us usable. Not remarkable in the eyes of the world, but marked by heaven's definition of greatness.

The markings of life we might have erased—our failures, scars, and moments of profound weakness—God intentionally preserves and transforms. In His economy, nothing is wasted. The rejections that humbled us, the struggles that taught us dependence, the broken places that birthed compassion—all become qualifications rather than disqualifications for His purposes. He chooses those who have learned to live under His covering—not because they chased influence, but because their identity is anchored so deeply in Him that they can carry responsibility without being corrupted by it.

This is the essence of remarkable living: surrender over striving, legacy over spotlight. Those most deeply marked by God's hand are those who've stopped striving to make a mark for themselves. They become vessels of clear light, not because they shine the brightest, but because they've stopped trying to reflect it back on themselves. Their lives speak loudly, not through accolades or applause, but through the people they've lifted, the burdens they've carried, and the unseen acts of love heaven alone records.

Spiritual and emotional maturity becomes visible when we can work without needing recognition, celebrate others getting credit for what we contributed, find joy in team success over personal acclaim, and serve with no expectation of acknowledgment. This is the path of the hidden hero—one who discovers fulfillment not in the spotlight, but in the shadow of the cross.

God begins His marking work when our ambitions lose steam. When we release the need to be seen or validated, He begins to inscribe a new story onto our lives. The disappointments, setbacks, and wounds we once wanted to erase become, in His hands, the very marks that set us apart. Not remarkable by the world's definition—but remarkable in the quiet, upside-down way of His kingdom.

In God's hands, nothing is wasted. The rejections that humbled us, the struggles that birthed dependence, the brokenness that taught us compassion—these become qualifications for His purpose.

> He entrusts influence to those whose identity is anchored in Him, not in acclaim.

Their lives shine, not from striving to be seen, but from surrendering to be used. True legacy isn't built through personal gain but through unseen love and quiet obedience that heaven alone records.

In working with others, I've recognized that an insatiable need to succeed causes us to bleed emotionally. The hard work required to reach the top may bring us accolades and status, but it ultimately leaves us empty and unfulfilled. Why? We were created to belong to God, not to ourselves.

When we live for our agenda, constantly chasing after "more," there is no true satisfaction. Facing this reality requires immense courage and humility. It means being willing to strip away the façade of pretense we have built and expose our raw, vulnerable places.

Only in this place of honest self-reflection can we begin to find the healing and wholeness our souls desperately crave. In embracing humility, we discover the deep satisfaction of belonging to Jesus.

Many leaders view team wins as diminishing their own influence. However, celebrating our team's achievements doesn't diminish our leadership; it validates it.

Leaders who publicly honor their team's successes don't reduce their own significance; they demonstrate their effectiveness. Authentic leadership is not about being the star but about creating stars.

When Keesha and I stepped into the roles of pastors at House of Prayer Church, the church began to grow, and we faced a choice that would reveal our true motives and priorities. Traditional wisdom said to keep our staff small, freeing up resources for programs—or even personal income.

I remember praying about this, sensing God's gentle guidance. What would serve the kingdom better—combining resources or investing in people? The Lord reminded us that His work was not about building our platform but raising up a generation of leaders who would extend far beyond what we could accomplish alone.

Our goal became building big people, not a big church. The more we leaned into that calling, the more we saw growth—not just in numbers, but in depth. People began to flourish in their gifts, not because we micromanaged them, but because we trusted them. We released them to serve, to lead, and to sometimes fail—and that space gave them room to grow.

It wasn't always easy. Letting go of control felt risky. But humility called us to believe in others, to invest in them, to equip them and cheer them on without needing to be at the center of everything. What we've seen is this: When you pour into others, your reach multiplies in ways no personal platform ever could.

The world tells us to climb. Jesus tells us to kneel.

The world says push your way to the front. Jesus says the first will be last.

The world says build your brand. Jesus says take up your cross.

The way of the kingdom is upside-down—and remarkably, it's the only way that truly satisfies.

When we live marked by humility, we stop striving to be remarkable in the eyes of others and instead become useful in the hands of God. It's not about being remembered. It's about being surrendered.

In the end, it won't matter how many people knew your name. What will matter is how well you reflected His.

Discussion Questions for Chapter 9: Remarkable

Let's Start Here:

We all carry "marks"—some seen, some unseen—that tell the story of where we've been. And often, those marks are what make us *remarkable*.

What's one of yours?

Maybe it's:

- A scar with a hilarious or meaningful backstory
- A quirky habit that traces back to a specific season of life
- A skill you picked up because of a hard (or weird) situation
- A personality trait shaped by your past
- A birthmark, freckle, or feature with a family legend behind it

We're not going deep here—just sharing the cool, funny, or unexpected ways life has "marked" us along the way.

1. Redefining Success

This chapter challenged the idea that external success—titles, accolades, influence—is what makes someone remarkable.

- Where have you been chasing a version of success that might be rooted in pride or pressure?
- What might it look like to redefine "success" through the lens of surrender?

2. The Risk of Letting Go

The author talked about releasing control as a leader—trusting others, giving space to fail, and cheering from the sidelines.

- Where are you still holding tight to control—whether in ministry, family, or relationships?
- What would it look like to lead with humility instead of fear?

3. Platform vs. People

God reminded Pastor Josh that ministry isn't about building a platform—it's about building people.

- Are there areas in your life where you've prioritized visibility over impact?

- Who has God placed in your life right now that you can invest in?

4. Measuring a Life Well Lived

The chapter ends by saying it's not about being remembered—it's about being surrendered.

- When you think about your legacy, what do you hope people remember about you?

- What would change if your goal was simply to reflect Christ well?

5. Real Satisfaction

Chasing "more" always leaves us empty. Humility, not striving, is where fulfillment is found.

- What's one area of your life where striving has replaced surrender?

- What would it mean to let go and let God redefine what's "enough" for you?

Further Reflection - The Power of Scars

The chapter reminds us that God doesn't erase our wounds—He transforms them.

- Is there a scar in your life that once felt like a source of shame but now points to God's grace?

- How might sharing that part of your story encourage someone else in the middle of their healing?

OLD TESTAMENT
SCRIPTURES ON HUMILITY

Explicit Humility Verses:

Numbers 12:3 NKJV—"Now the man Moses was very meek, above all men who were on the face of the earth."

2 Chronicles 7:14 NKJV—"If My people who are called by My name will humble themselves, and pray and seek My face, and turn from their wicked ways, then I will hear from heaven, and will forgive their sin and heal their land."

2 Chronicles 12:6–7 NKJV—"So the leaders of Israel and the king humbled themselves; and they said, 'The Lord is righteous.' Now when the Lord saw that they humbled themselves, the word of the Lord came to Shemaiah, saying, 'They have humbled themselves; therefore I will not destroy them, but I will grant them some deliverance.'"

2 Chronicles 32:26 NKJV—"Then Hezekiah humbled himself for the pride of his heart, he and the inhabitants of Jerusalem, so that the wrath of the Lord did not come upon them in the days of Hezekiah."

2 Chronicles 33:12 NKJV—"Now when he was in affliction, he implored the Lord his God, and humbled himself greatly before the God of his fathers."

2 Chronicles 34:27 NKJV—"'Because your heart was tender, and you humbled yourself before God when you heard His words against this place and against its inhabitants, and you humbled yourself before Me, and you tore your clothes and wept before Me, I also have heard you,' says the Lord."

Psalm 25:9 NKJV—"The humble He guides in justice, and the humble He teaches His way."

Psalm 34:2 NKJV—"My soul shall make its boast in the Lord; the humble shall hear of it and be glad."

Psalm 34:18 NKJV—"The Lord is near to those who have a broken heart, and saves such as have a contrite spirit."

Psalm 51:17 NKJV—"The sacrifices of God are a broken spirit, a broken and a contrite heart—these, O God, You will not despise."

Psalm 69:32 NKJV—"The humble shall see this and be glad; and you who seek God, your hearts shall live."

Psalm 138:6 NKJV—"Though the Lord is on high, yet He regards the lowly; but the proud He knows from afar."

Psalm 147:6 NKJV—"The Lord lifts up the humble; He casts the wicked down to the ground."

Psalm 149:4 NKJV—"For the Lord takes pleasure in His people; He will beautify the humble with salvation."

Proverbs 3:34 NKJV—"Surely He scorns the scornful, but gives grace to the humble."

Proverbs 11:2 NKJV—"When pride comes, then comes shame; but with the humble is wisdom."

Proverbs 15:33 NKJV—"The fear of the Lord is the instruction of wisdom, and before honor is humility."

Proverbs 16:18–19 NKJV—"Pride goes before destruction, and a haughty spirit before a fall. Better to be of a humble spirit with the lowly, than to divide the spoil with the proud."

Proverbs 18:12 NKJV—"Before destruction the heart of man is haughty, and before honor is humility."

Proverbs 22:4 NKJV—"By humility and the fear of the Lord are riches and honor and life."

Proverbs 25:6–7 NKJV—"Do not exalt yourself in the presence of the king, and do not stand in the place of the great; for it is better that he say to you, 'Come up here,' than that you should be put lower in the presence of the prince."

Proverbs 27:2 NKJV—"Let another man praise you, and not your own mouth; a stranger, and not your own lips."

Proverbs 29:23 NKJV—"A man's pride will bring him low, but the humble in spirit will retain honor."

Isaiah 57:15 NKJV—"For thus says the High and Lofty One who inhabits eternity, whose name is Holy: 'I dwell in the high and holy place, with him who has a contrite and humble spirit, to revive the spirit of the humble, and to revive the heart of the contrite ones.'"

Isaiah 66:2 NKJV—"'For all those things My hand has made, and all those things exist,' says the Lord. 'But on this one will I look: on him who is poor and of a contrite spirit, and who trembles at My word.'"

Micah 6:8 NKJV—"He has shown you, O man, what is good; and what does the Lord require of you but to do justly, to love mercy, and to walk humbly with your God?"

Zephaniah 2:3 NKJV—"Seek the Lord, all you meek of the earth, who have upheld His justice. Seek righteousness, seek humility. It may be that you will be hidden in the day of the Lord's anger."

NEW TESTAMENT
SCRIPTURES ON HUMILITY

Jesus' Teachings:

Matthew 5:3 NKJV—"Blessed are the poor in spirit, for theirs is the kingdom of heaven."

Matthew 11:29 NKJV—"Take My yoke upon you and learn from Me, for I am gentle and lowly in heart, and you will find rest for your souls."

Matthew 18:3–4 NKJV—"And said, 'Assuredly, I say to you, unless you are converted and become as little children, you will by no means enter the kingdom of heaven. Therefore whoever humbles himself as this little child is the greatest in the kingdom of heaven.'"

Matthew 20:26–28 NKJV—"Yet it shall not be so among you; but whoever desires to become great among you, let him be your servant. And whoever desires to be first among you, let him be your slave— just as the Son of Man did not come to be served, but to serve, and to give His life a ransom for many."

Matthew 23:12 NKJV—"And whoever exalts himself will be humbled, and he who humbles himself will be exalted."

Mark 9:35 NKJV—"And He sat down, called the twelve, and said to them, 'If anyone desires to be first, he shall be last of all and servant of all.'"

Mark 10:43–44 NKJV—"Yet it shall not be so among you; but whoever desires to become great among you shall be your servant. And whoever of you desires to be first shall be slave of all."

Luke 9:48 NKJV—"And said to them, 'Whoever receives this little child in My name receives Me; and whoever receives Me receives Him who sent Me. For he who is least among you all will be great.'"

Luke 14:11 NKJV—"For whoever exalts himself will be humbled, and he who humbles himself will be exalted."

Luke 18:14 NKJV—"I tell you, this man went down to his house justified rather than the other; for everyone who exalts himself will be humbled, and he who humbles himself will be exalted."

Luke 22:26 NKJV—"But not so among you; on the contrary, he who is greatest among you, let him be as the younger, and he who governs as he who serves."

John 13:14–17 NKJV—"If I then, your Lord and Teacher, have washed your feet, you also ought to wash one another's feet. For I have given you an example, that you should do as I have done to you. Most assuredly, I say to you, a servant is not greater than his master; nor is he who is sent greater than he who sent him. If you know these things, blessed are you if you do them."

Paul's Writings:

Romans 12:3 NKJV—"For I say, through the grace given to me, to everyone who is among you, not to think of himself more highly than he ought to think, but to think soberly, as God has dealt to each one a measure of faith."

Romans 12:16 NKJV—"Be of the same mind toward one another. Do not set your mind on high things, but associate with the humble. Do not be wise in your own opinion."

1 Corinthians 1:27–29 NKJV—"But God has chosen the foolish things of the world to put to shame the wise, and God has chosen the weak things of the world to put to shame the things which are mighty; and the base things of the world and the things which are despised God has chosen, and the things which are not, to bring to nothing the things that are, that no flesh should glory in His presence."

1 Corinthians 4:7 NKJV—"For who makes you differ from another? And what do you have that you did not receive? Now if you did indeed receive it, why do you boast as if you had not received it?"

2 Corinthians 12:9–10 NKJV—"And He said to me, 'My grace is sufficient for you, for My strength is made perfect in weakness.' Therefore most gladly I will rather boast in my infirmities, that the power of Christ may rest upon me. Therefore I take pleasure in infirmities, in reproaches, in needs, in persecutions, in distresses, for Christ's sake. For when I am weak, then I am strong."

Galatians 6:3 NKJV—"For if anyone thinks himself to be something, when he is nothing, he deceives himself."

Ephesians 4:2 NKJV—"With all lowliness and gentleness, with longsuffering, bearing with one another in love."

Philippians 2:3–4 NKJV—"Let nothing be done through selfish ambition or conceit, but in lowliness of mind let each esteem others better than himself. Let each of you look out not only for his own interests, but also for the interests of others."

Philippians 2:5–8 NKJV—"Let this mind be in you which was also in Christ Jesus, who, being in the form of God, did not consider it robbery to be equal with God, but made Himself of no reputation, taking the form of a bondservant, and coming in the likeness of men. And being found in appearance as a man, He humbled Himself and became obedient to the point of death, even the death of the cross."

Colossians 3:12 NKJV—"Therefore, as the elect of God, holy and beloved, put on tender mercies, kindness, humility, meekness, longsuffering."

James 1:9–10 NKJV—"Let the lowly brother glory in his exaltation, but the rich in his humiliation, because as a flower of the field he will pass away."

James 3:13 NKJV—"Who is wise and understanding among you? Let him show by good conduct that his works are done in the meekness of wisdom."

James 4:6 NKJV—"But He gives more grace. Therefore He says: 'God resists the proud, but gives grace to the humble.'"

James 4:10 NKJV—"Humble yourselves in the sight of the Lord, and He will lift you up."

Peter's Writings:

1 Peter 3:8 NKJV—"Finally, all of you be of one mind, having compassion for one another; love as brothers, be tenderhearted, be courteous."

1 Peter 5:5–6 NKJV—"Likewise you younger people, submit yourselves to your elders. Yes, all of you be submissive to one another, and be clothed with humility, for 'God resists the proud, but gives grace to the humble.' Therefore humble yourselves under the mighty hand of God, that He may exalt you in due time."

Additional Key Verses (Mixed Versions):

Deuteronomy 8:2 NIV—"Remember how the Lord your God led you all the way in the wilderness these forty years, to humble and test you in order to know what was in your heart, whether or not you would keep his commands."

Job 22:29 NIV—"When people are brought low and you say, 'Lift them up!' then he will save the downcast."

Daniel 4:37 KJV—"Now I Nebuchadnezzar praise and extol and honour the King of heaven, all whose works are truth, and his ways judgment: and those that walk in pride he is able to abase."

Zephaniah 3:12 ESV—"But I will leave in your midst a people humble and lowly. They shall seek refuge in the name of the Lord."

1 Corinthians 15:9–10 ESV—"For I am the least of the apostles, unworthy to be called an apostle, because I persecuted the church of God. But by the grace of God I am what I am, and his grace toward me was not in vain."

ACKNOWLEDGMENTS

To my beautiful wife, Keesha—thank you for your unwavering support, your wisdom, and your constant encouragement. You have walked with me through these lessons, helping me wrestle with them not only in my own life but also in our marriage, in raising our children, and in leading God's church. This journey would not be the same without you.

To my children, Jensen and Miley—you inspire me every day. Jensen, I believe with all my heart that you will one day model the mark of the least in a way that profoundly honors God and makes a difference in this world. Miley, as you lead in worship, you reveal the character of humility and the power of God in a way that moves hearts. I am so proud of y'all.

To my father, Bishop Ronnie Melancon—thank you for modeling what it means to embrace humble beginnings and for showing me that God's greatest gifts often come wrapped in simplicity. Your legacy of faithfulness continues to shape my understanding of true leadership.

To Raymond Woodward—thank you for your wisdom, friendship, and for writing the foreword that so beautifully captures the heart of this message. Your words carry weight because your life carries the mark of humility.

To my faithful beta readers—Tony Rivera, Ann Buisson, and Desiree Percle—thank you for your honest feedback, your encouragement, and for helping refine these words before they reached the world. Your insights made this book stronger and clearer.

To Chermaine Stein—thank you for helping me start this book, along with countless hours of support, encouragement, and input. Your voice and insight have made this work stronger. Your dedication behind the scenes has been invaluable.

To Mandy Holloway—your gift for shaping ideas and giving structure to my creativity has made this book something truly special. I am forever grateful for how you helped bring this vision to life. It wouldn't be on pages without your genius.

To my church family at House of Prayer—thank you for your constant support, loyalty, and prayers. It is my deepest desire to be as much of a blessing to you as you have been to me.

And to every reader who will walk through these pages—thank you for having the courage to examine your own heart. May you discover, as I have, that the way up is down, and that carrying the mark of the least is the greatest honor of all.

"He must increase, but I must decrease" (John 3:30 KJV).

ABOUT THE AUTHOR

Pastor Josh Melancon serves as Lead Pastor of House of Prayer's Central Campus in Thibodaux, Louisiana, where he also oversees the Larose campus. Under his leadership, these congregations have grown into thriving communities committed to discipleship and Christ-centered leadership.

Josh is the author of *Church Junkies* and a contributing writer to *Love's Letters*. His devotional on the YouVersion Bible App has been completed by over 1,000 readers. He speaks regularly at conferences and churches across the US and recently led leadership workshops during a ministry trip to the United Kingdom with his wife, Keesha.

Mark of the Least is Josh's most personal work to date—a transparent reflection on how God reshaped his ministry and identity from the inside out, calling him from platform-driven ambition to surrendered service.

Josh and Keesha live in southern Louisiana and are the proud parents of two young adults, Jensen and Miley.

ALSO BY JOSH MELANCON

Church Junkies
Breaking Free From Religious Addiction

Is church the last place you'd expect to find joy? Whether you're burnt out, curious, or still showing up out of habit, *Church Junkies* helps you:

- Rediscover God's design for genuine community
- Identify the inner obstacles that keep you stuck
- Trade survival-mode faith for a life that thrives

With candor and humor, Josh calls out the junk while charting a path to emotional and spiritual wholeness.

Free 7-day devotional now on YouVersion.
Search Church Junkies in the Bible app.

CONNECT WITH PASTOR JOSH

Move from *least* to *leader* without losing humility

Leadership Coaching

Clarify your calling and lead from a place of surrender—not striving. One-to-one sessions help you align gifting with God's purpose and build influence that lasts. *Book a complimentary discovery call today.*

Marriage Conferences (with Keesha Melancon)

Turn "two becoming one" from theory into practice. Through stories, Scripture, and the Primal Question framework, the Melancons equip couples to communicate deeply and fight for—not with—each other. *Invite us to your next retreat or weekend intensive.*

Leadership Training for Teams

Workshops that flip the usual org-chart: people over platforms, service over status. Equip your staff to lead like Jesus and watch culture shift. *Request the training overview PDF.*

Website **melanconministries.com**
Email **josh@melanconministries.com**
Social **@MelanconMinistries**

Let's pursue greatness through leastness—together.

GREAT BOOKS

ARE EVEN BETTER WHEN THEY'RE SHARED!

Help other readers find this one:

- Post a review at your favorite online bookseller

- Post a picture on a social media account and share why you enjoyed it

- Send a note to a friend who would also love it—or better yet, give them a copy

MELANCON
MINISTRIES

www.ingramcontent.com/pod-product-compliance
Lightning Source LLC
Chambersburg PA
CBHW070339130626
46556CB00007B/2942